D0592559

You Have My Word

from the same authors

You Can't Have Your Kayak and Heat It!
Upon My Word!
Take My Word For It
Oh, My Word
collected together as
The Complete and Utter 'My Word!' Collection

Frank Muir and Denis Norden

You Have My Word

A fifth collection of stories from 'My Word!'
a panel game devised by
Edward J. Mason and Tony Shryane

Methuen London

First published in 1989
by Methuen London
Michelin House, 81 Fulham Road, London SW3 6RB

© 1989 by Frank Muir and Denis Norden

Printed and bound in Great Britain by
Mackays of Chatham PLC, Chatham, Kent

ISBN 0 413 61810 2

A CIP catalogue record for this book
is available from the British Library

Contents

Once more unto the breach, dear friends, once more

William Shakespeare
Henry the Fifth, Act Three, Scene one

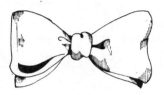

THE loss of a dear one was celebrated in Edwardian days by tying up the front-door knocker with a strip of black velvet to quieten the impact of visitors calling. Our recent bereavement could not be marked in such a manner, if only because we had unscrewed our front-door knocker many years ago. It was a cast-iron job representing a lion with a ring in its mouth and was of enormous weight. The last time a visitor arrived at the front door sufficiently strong to lift the iron ring and let it fall, a shock-wave ripped through the ground floor, kitchen cupboards flew open, one cat succumbed to hysterics and the other to worse, a mirror cracked right across, pictures fell off the wall and the dogs crammed themselves into the corner under the stairs, paws over their ears and moaning piteously. We dislodged them later with the garden rake.

But knockerless or not, due to the zeal of a certain Policewoman Twisk, my lady wife and I have been mourning the loss of a beloved and irreplaceable family friend – our Dennis (no, not *him*. Denis, like Finchley but unlike Minneapolis, spells his name with one N). No, the dear departed was our Dennis lawnmower.

When, some thirty-six years ago, my wife and I took over the couple of acres of rough in the village of Thorpe (the best end of Surrey) which is now our lovely home, a lawnmower capable of crunching up gravel and discarded horseshoes and bits of barbed wire as well as grass was vital if we were to reduce the acreage of farmland tussocks into a svelte lawn. A chap advised a Dennis.

A Dennis, this wise chap said, was a lawnmower which was lightly converted by Mr Dennis, an entrepreneur of genius, from a job lot of first-world war army tanks. It is a heavy machine – a third of a ton – which if left on wet grass will sink down to its starting-handle in the soft earth, but it is most certainly tough.

I put a small-ad in the *Gardener's Weekly*, did a deal, and a month later a farmer arrived with my Dennis on a low-loader. I questioned him closely and it became clear that the small price he was asking was due to the fact that nobody had been able to start the machine for eight years. The nearest had been a heavyweight Royal Marine boy-friend of his daughter who had swung the handle powerfully but unwisely. The Dennis had coughed and the swinger had been swung in a lazy arc over the milking-sheds.

My friend George, who understands bits of metal, took the machine to pieces. He found that there was no sparking-plug in the one huge cylinder so it had become a home for a family of field-mice. Also, the reason why the engine would not start was because something called the magneto had rusted into a solid block. George cleaned and sharpened and replaced and filed and put everything together and it started.

Small motor mowers in those days either buzzed with a thin noise like a petulant mosquito, or hummed quietly before suddenly eating their own umbilical cord with a blue flash. The Dennis simply throbbed richly; its enormous cylinder producing an unhurried thump like a vintage Bentley. 'Dum-dum-dum-dum' it went. And the power of it. Anybody under ten stone who let the clutch in a bit sharpish was whisked off his feet and carried along clinging to the crossbar and fluttering like a pennant in Cowes week.

It was our first food-processor. One summer we had to feed forty local boy-scouts. I found that by jacking up the mower and sliding underneath the blades the drip-tray used for draining dirty oil from the car sump (giving the tray a good wipe with an old newspaper first, of course), I could drop whole lettuces, boiled eggs, tomatoes, etc., into the whirling blades and cut up four or five bucketfuls of *salade niçoise* in as many minutes. And by lowering the mower until the blades were almost touching the drip-tray and running it at tickover, I could mix the egg yolks and trickle in the oil to knock up a very passable gallon of mayonnaise.

And ironing the drawing-room curtains. I used a couple of blowlamps to heat up the mower's cylinder until it was really hot, laid the curtains out on the crazy paving, dampened them with the garden sprinkler and, in a cloud of steam, rode the machine slowly backwards and forwards over them. They were beautifully ironed, although I resolved that next time I would weed the crazy paving first.

I say 'rode the machine' because the Dennis had a seat. And that perhaps was its undoing.

Last week I learned of a small problem in the village. The three tiny, frail and very old Potter sisters wanted to go and see the fourth Potter sister, Winifred, whose birthday it was, but they had no car. And a car was not much use anyway as Winifred lived in an old cottage on Chobham Common at the end of half a mile of footpath. Could I help in any way? I think the village was hoping I would hire a helicopter.

The answer, of course, was The Mower.

From the vicar I borrowed some old hassocks which were waiting for a retread and lined the mower's grassbox with these. Yesterday afternoon the three old ladies arrived, neat and trim, clutching their jars of chutney and tins of home-made birthday cakes. I helped them into the grassbox and they made themselves comfortable, like churchmice, among the hassocks. They held on to the front of the grassbox with gloved hands, their heads just showing above.

Off we chugged. The ten horsepower engine of the Dennis was undismayed by the load. Across Thorpe Green we went, the little ladies giving charming, Queen Mother-like waves to passing, goggling, motorists. Up Sandhills Lane we went with no trouble and into a left turn at the lights.

This was Trumps Green Road and downhill, with a sharp turn at the bottom which had an ancient brick railway bridge straddling it.

'Stop!'

I declutched and brought the mower to an emergency halt. In front of it stood the massive form of Policewoman Twisk, hand upraised.

'There has been a robbery. I am comandeering your vehicle to give chase to the malefactor. Kindly vacate the driving-seat!'

'But you couldn't overtake a bicycle on a mower, let alone a getaway car,' I pointed out.

'The malefactor is not in a car,' said Policewoman Twisk. 'It's that little Jason Snell on his skateboard again. He's nicked a copy of *Playboy* from the paper shop and made off with it. In the name of the law! . . .' And she elbowed me off the machine.

'My little ladies!' I called out as she let in the clutch and thundered off down the hill. 'Be careful of my little ladies!'

I knew in my bones she was going too fast as she approached the bend at the bottom of the hill. She began to slide and fought to regain control but with a hideous sound of tearing metal the mower slewed round and crashed sideways into the brick bridge.

The old ladies were fine. They were tossed about a bit among the hassocks but unhurt and thought it was all part of the journey. Best of all a squad car arrived and took them off to the sister Winifred's cottage, the officers carrying the ladies the last part of the journey piggyback.

But the mower – our mower – our gallant and faithful friend – was no more. It was now scrap; the mainframe snapped, the once magnificent cylinder cracked across, the roller broken into many parts.

Looking back on it, my wife and I cannot find it in our hearts to blame Policewoman Twisk. The police have a difficult enough job to do combating vicious crime in country areas. It is just that we had such bad luck in losing a friend.

One could come to terms with an impersonal loss, like the police commandeering one's car and accidently driving that into the bridge. But –

One's mower into the bridge, dear friends, one's *mower*.

Never underestimate the power of a woman

Advertising slogan

I T WASN'T much of a kiss. Not compared to what I'd been expecting. So briefly had her lips brushed against mine, I was in two minds whether it rated even half a *!* in my diary. In fact, I can remember thinking to myself, 'I've had more sensation putting my tongue across the two sticking-up metal bits of a torch battery.'

But still . . . At the age of sixteen, to find oneself in any kind of mouth to mouth conjunction with, wait for it, Jocasta Yarborough! The only equivalent I could summon up was the man who broke the bank at Monte Carlo drawing the winning ticket in the Irish Sweepstake.

Feeling that it was up to me to break the silence, I said, 'Gulp!' The word, I mean. Although I had intended it to be the kind of whimsical, one-eyebrow-cocked compliment currently being used to great effect by a Hollywood role model of mine called Franchot Tone, a failure of spit in the course of the vowel sound made it come out unnervingly shrill.

Jocasta appeared not to notice. 'Let's not waste any more time,' she said. 'Get your clothes off.'

At sixteen, one can be woefully unsure of one's luck. 'Are you absolutely positive about this?' I asked. She shrugged, a component of her body language that always had an unsettling effect on me. Only the previous night, my diary entry had been, 'When Jocasta shrugs, it initiates a movement like a breeze across a cornfield.'

'Get 'em off,' she said and left the bedroom.

As I removed my clothes, I could not help reflecting on the strange course of our relationship. At the Tennis Club I had long worshipped her lithe figure from afar, but there had been no opportunity to do so from, as it were, a-near till the afternoon I was drawn as her partner in the Mixed Doubles. Though recognising immediately that her station in life was way above mine – hers was the only racquet in the Club that had every one of its strings – I only discovered the exact dimensions of the gulf between us when Pud Wilson took me to one side.

'Before you get in too deep there,' said Pud, who was one of the Club's Singles Champions and therefore a girl to be trusted, 'Just bear in mind that she's a Yarborough. And you must have heard of the Yarborough family.'

Who hadn't heard of the Yarborough family, our neighbourhood's only link with the nobility. An ancestor of Lady Yarborough, Jocasta's mother, had reputedly been principal lookout for Lady Godiva, while her father's side of the family could trace its lineage back as far as the Officers' Mess Dance that followed the Battle of Hastings. Jocasta, therefore, had been born with not just a silver spoon in her mouth but more or less the entire twelve-piece dinner service.

Daunting as those trappings of rank and privilege were, I did not let them over-awe me. On two pages of our best pad of lined notepaper, I wrote her a letter saying, 'Dear Miss Honorable Jocasta, Would you deign me the honour of having dinner with me some p.m., or even a.m. should such be mutually convenient. Your obedient servant,'.

After three weeks had passed without any acknowledgement, I once again telephoned Pud, who gladly obtained Jocasta's telephone number for me in exchange for a pipeful of my father's tobacco. Jocasta rang off the moment she heard my voice but I refused to allow myself to become discouraged and telephoned again. Three times a day. For four months. Finally, any reluctance she may have felt was abandoned and she not only spoke to me but agreed to come out to dinner.

Determined to spare no expense, I took her to the most elegant restaurant I knew and as we were carrying our trays back to the counter, I asked the question my heart had for so long been rehearsing.

'Joke,' I said, employing my own cherished diminutive of her name, 'will you be my girl?'

She said, 'Don't be ludicrous.'

'But why not?' I cried.

'Because I am upper-class,' she answered. 'While you and your entire family are rubbish.'

'Only socially and financially,' I said hotly. 'Please, won't you at least grant me reason to hope?'

She tossed her head – that yellow mass of hair with occasional glints of gold in it, like sunshine on cornflakes – then her eyes suddenly narrowed. 'Tell you what,' she said. 'Why don't you come to tea on Saturday and I'll introduce you to Pa. Pass muster with him, and you're in with a chance.'

All of that was going through my mind as I placed the last of my garments across the Chippendale wash-basin. On my arrival, Jocasta had explained that, as is so often the case with high-born families, the Yarboroughs were keen naturists. As token of their natural superiority, it was their habit to take Saturday afternoon tea in the garden completely unclothed – something they knew the lower orders were unable to emulate, because not only are their gardens small and overlooked, but they grow up with no inherited talent for balancing hot tea on the naked lap.

From afar, I heard Jocasta's voice summoning me with a private pet name I had insisted she, in her turn, should devise for me. 'Yobbo,' she called. 'Pa says the tea's getting cold.'

So, gingerly – and naked as a peeled egg – I went downstairs, into the drawing room and out through the French windows on to a lawn that looked as though it had been trimmed with nail-scissors and spirit-level.

You know, I wouldn't be at all surprised if you haven't anticipated me here. They were, of course, fully clothed. All of them. Her father, her mother, her two grandparents . . . the visiting bishop.

The one thing to be said for my youthful humiliations is that they do tend to provide some form of guidance for the young men of today. In this case, it's a valuable piece of advice for anyone on his way to a first meeting with some unfamiliar female's father.

The golden rule, if my experience is anything to go by, would appear to be –

'Never undress to meet the pa of a woman.'

Open confession is good for the soul

Proverb

I HAVE a passion for proverbs like the above. The truth reduced to a cough and a spit as you might put it (though *The Oxford Book of Proverbs* doesn't as yet). Proverbs, together with their cousins the Aphorisms, Maxims and Saws, have been a formative factor in my intellectual development ever since I wore my gloves round my neck on a piece of string and ate plasticine for an hour a day at Mrs Pavett's Mixed Infants.

It has long been my dream to invent a proverbial saying so wise and useful that it would be published in all the anthologies and my name would be in the index between '*Muggleton*, Lodowick; English fanatic' and *Mulford*, Elisha; Pa., philosophical writer'.

And I tried hard some years ago. The first proverb I invented, which I must admit was a trifle flawed, ran:

'More than enough is better than less than nothing at all.'

It reads well but the flaw, which you may have noticed, is that it doesn't actually mean anything. This is not good practice in proverb compiling because only the Bible is allowed to get away with that (e.g., 'Sufficient unto the day is the evil thereof.' Eh?).

I thought a domestic approach might be productive, so after some research I discovered a home truth which I preserved like a fly in amber in a carefully balanced sentence:

'Never rest a warm baby on a cold slab!'

Nobody showed the slightest interest in saying it, let alone printing it. Was I perhaps being *too* brief, *too* witty? I decided to concentrate on producing something more leisurely, a brilliant thought expressed in a more philosophical and unhurried rhetoric in the style of Demosthenes rather than Ben Elton. Inspiration struck one Tuesday morning. The proverb, when honed and polished, proved to be a corker. It went:

'However fortunate you are in your pathway through life's travails always remember that it is the duty of those to whom fortune has been granted to be as kind and helpful as possible to those unfortunates who unfortunately have had the misfortune to be less fortunate than those whose fortune it has been to be more fortunate than those less fortunate than themselves.'

Sings, doesn't it?

But, incredible though it may seem to you, it fell dead from my pen. Nobody sought to quote it. Even after repeated phone calls, The *Reader's Digest* evinced no interest in printing it as an example of Picturesque Speech. I sent it to the compiler of the *The Faber Book of Familiar Phrases and Sayings* every week for a year (the post can be so unreliable) but all I got back eventually was a slip with a most *un*familiar phrase or saying written on it. I had never previously met two of the words, which were quite short. I showed the saying to some people at the village shop hoping for elucidation: Fred behind the counter said 'Christ!' and a quietly-spoken lady dropped a box of a dozen new-laid eggs (number twos at that).

The years rolled by and I was beginning to think that I was never going to achieve immortality through inventing a proverb when serendipity struck. Serendipity, I need hardly remind you, is a word coined by the late Horace Walpole to describe something nice happening by accident while you are trying to achieve something quite different. Like running over your mother-in-law after volunteering to back your wife's car into a parking space.

My wife and I had no way of knowing what that something nice which was going to befall us was that Friday when we took a cab to the Highlands of Scotland.

It was not our intention to go to Scotland. It had been a dreadfully tiring day for both of us. There is a large corner of our garden where nothing will grow; the soil is far too heavy and sticky and we have never had a potato out of it larger than a pea: so we double-dug the whole soggy mess, a back-breaking task not helped by the fact that we only had one spade between us so one of us had to dig with a soup spoon.

15

Reeling with exhaustion by mid-afternoon, we caught a train up to Waterloo, slumped into a cab on the rank and asked the driver to take us to Holborn (we were due to attend the Annual General Meeting there of the Society for the Reform of Annual General Meetings. Our annual treat).

'Well, guv',' I heard him say, 'Thy blood be upon thine own bonce, as the poet hath it. But if that's whatcher want, 'Olborn, 'ere we come!' I thought at the time it was an odd thing to come out with but I was too exhausted to worry.

We were both woken by the cab jolting to a halt and a cheery cry from the driver of 'Ere we are then, wakey-wakey!'

We stumbled out of the cab. 'How much on the meter,' I mumbled, fumbling in my back pocket for the five pound note.

'Four 'undred and eighty-six pounds, fifty pee,' said the cabby. 'Not counting tip'.

I reeled and almost fell.

'What!? Where on earth have you taken us?' I quavered.

'Where you asked me to take you, matey – Oban.'

With an awful sinking feeling I realised how similar were pronunciations of the words 'Oban' and ''Olborn'. 'You mean that we're in the Scottish Highlands?'

'That's right, guv. Oban. The Port of Scotland. Gateway to the 'ighlands. Read that on a sign just as dawn was breaking.'

What to do? We had no money to pay the cabby his fare. It was a nightmare. In fact, the cabby was a sport and took it all as a bit of an adventure, which is more than my wife and I were able to do what with trying to work out how to get home and the worry about how the voting went at the AGM of the S. for the R. of AGMs – i.e., did that trouble-maker, the Rev. Theo Usher, win a seat at last on the Steering Committee?

As the sun rose higher, the streets began to fill with people and we found that it was the last day of Oban's Carnival Week. There was music; young people danced in the streets and old people sat in shelters and passed remarks.

From my fiver I bought the three of us some sandwiches and coffee. The Cabby also had two lots of candy-floss and a Cherry Ciderette.

It was in the afternoon that I saw a booth on the promenade with a sign on it GRAND DRAW – First Prize: £1,000 !!!!! One Hundred

Other Prizes !!!! Tickets £1 only !!! Prizes drawn at 6pm by Miss Phyllis Grist, Oban's own Television Celebrity and Fire-Eater.

The answer! A thousand pounds would pay for the taxi's return trip! I dug in my pockets. I had £1.19 left. Heart in mouth, I bought a draw ticket. The cabby, not to be left out of the fun, bought one for himself.

At six o'clock, the whole town seemed to have gathered on the front for the Grand Draw. Breaths were baited. Conversation dried up. Silence fell as the Fire-Eater made her way to the microphone to announce the results.

Suffice it to say that our cabby won the first prize of £1,000.

My wife and I did not leave empty-handed; we won the ninety-fourth prize – a quantity of Old Scottish sweeties. When we turned up at the sweetshop to collect our prize we found it was not a selection of exciting traditional Scottish sweetmeats like toffee-haggis on a stick, or crystallised thistles, but a load of out-of-date sweets which had perished; Edinburgh rock that was like granite, marshmallows which had gone as hard as pebbles, licorice allsorts like bullets – half a ton of the stuff. As it was delivered at their expense there was nothing we could do but accept it and it arrived at our home a week later. What on earth were we to do with a lorry load of what seemed to be Highland hard-core?

It was then that serendipity took over. The cabby wrote to say that the money he had won covered the fare and he had so enjoyed himself that he would not dream of taking a penny from us.

And my wife took a long look at the lorryload and inspiration dawned. 'Of *course!*' she said. 'That is just the roughage we need to dig into that heavy corner of the garden to break up and drain the soil!'

She was right, too. The following year our potatoes were the size of grapefruit, our sweet corn was sweet as a nut and as high as an elephant's eye or any other bit of him, and our tomatoes were worth a guinea apiece.

And the lesson to be learnt from our horticultural triumph gave me, at long last, my posterity-worthy proverb:

'Oban confectionary's good for the soil!'

It'll Be All Right On The Night

Title of a TV programme,
derived from an old theatrical incantation

SOMETHING else I've been meaning to tell you
. . . I've just bought a new car! Well, it was about time. The old
one had reached a stage in its life-cycle when I either had to trade it
in or have it put down. Its front number-plate was perpetually
askew, both wing-mirrors had gone sort of limp and the quantity of
smoke issuing from the exhaust gave you the feeling you were
driving a crop-sprayer.

Why did I hang on to it so long? For the same reason I always
tend to put off buying a new car: because my ignorance as regards
the automobile and its innards is practically total. (All I know about
an engine is that there has to be one.) Consequently, whenever I get
into a showroom, I have no idea what to ask for. I wind a few
electric windows up and down, or kick some tyres here and there,
but when the salesman comes over and starts enquiring what kind
of car I have in mind, I never rise to anything more technical than
'A red one'.

This time, though, I was able to be much more precise about my
requirements, my family having decided that I should try a Japanese
car for a change. There wasn't a red one in stock, unfortunately,
but the Montreal Blue featured all manner of exciting things in the
way of gee-whiz gadgetry; so many, in fact, that the salesman felt
obliged to climb in the front beside me and offer a swift guided tour
round the various knobs and switches.

Oddly enough, I had no difficulty coming to terms with most of
them. The problem came when he indicated a button down on my
left somewhere and said, 'This is another distinctive feature of the
Honda Accord. It controls your Headlamp Washer and Wiper
Unit.'

I said, 'My what unit?'

He said, 'Headlamp Washer and Wiper. Suppose you're driving along and suddenly decide your headlamps could do with a wash and a wipe. You just give this button a quick press.'

I said, 'Do you know something? In all the more than two score years I have been driving the roads of this world that thought has never once entered my head. What's more,' I continued, 'Of all the millions of abusive phrases other motorists have yelled at me during those years, not one of them has ever yelled, "Get your headlamps washed and wiped!"'

They're very smooth, these car salesmen. This one had an approach somewhere between Donald Sinden and a papal nuncio. With a shrug so slight as to be almost imperceptible, he said, 'Sir, had there not been evidence of considerable consumer demand for a Headlamp Washer and Wiper Unit, Honda would not have installed one.'

That pulled me up short. 'Are you telling me,' I said, 'are you actually telling me that's all you have to do to get some hitherto undreamt-of piece of car-gadgetry installed? Just show a manufacturer there's a consumer demand for it?'

'A *mass* consumer demand,' he corrected. 'Now, are we sure we wouldn't like a tiny bit more instruction on distinguishing the right indicator from the left?'

But I was already miles away. (Mentally, I mean. The acceleration on Hondas isn't *that* good.) Something had suddenly occured to me. If the only thing required to effect improvements in a car was mass consumer demand – why not enlist the *My Word!* audience?

Think about it. If all the people who listen to this programme are prepared to speak with one voice, there are enough of us to change the entire face of today's motor-car!

Of course, the first thing we'll have to decide is what kind of new features we want from the manufacturers. Just to make sure they don't waste any more dashboard buttons on headlamp hygiene, let me list the kind of additional items I'd like to see them installing.

We can start with some fairly simple devices, such as a windscreen wiper that will automatically switch itself off when you are going under a bridge; or a Teflon Thigh Spray that can be applied in hot weather to prevent you sticking to the upholstery when you're wearing tennis shorts. But then I think we should go on to some improvements that would really put technology at the service of the road user.

19

One I feel sure all my fellow-drivers would appreciate is a special sound-activated thingummy that would operate if you are at the traffic lights and the moment they go green, the man in the car behind starts blasting on his hooter. What I have in mind is some kind of *sensor*, so that at the first onset of sound from the rear, a mechanically propelled arm shoots out from your boot and squirts boiling yoghurt all over his windscreen.

Another device that could reduce stress among motorists would be some kind of locating instrument, for use when you've put your car in one of those enormous multi-storey car parks and come back to find you have absolutely no idea where you left it. I have a notion that the answer might be a variation of the remote-control gadget used for the TV set. You would keep it in your pocket or briefcase at all times, so that on your return to the car park, you could simply remove it and press one of its buttons. Whereupon, your car would draw attention to its location by flashing all its lights on and off, while a special high-pitched siren attached to your roof would emit a recognisable and pre-programmed sequence of long and short shrieks.

I do, of course, accept that if all the other parked motorists had one of these as well, things would get a bit noisy – but at this stage I am only indicating what the requirement is. (Those car manufacturers can't expect me to do *all* their thinking for them.)

Assuming that *My Word!* listeners now agree that every one of these suggestions would improve the quality of life on our roads, what must our next step be? Well, having created a mass consumer demand, we must now proceed to *organise* it.

You will not be surprised to learn I have thought long and hard about that, too. The plan is as follows: every evening next week, each listener will send a letter suggesting the above improvements to all the car manufacturers. And, in view of the fact that maximum consumer impact will only be achieved if all those letters arrive simultaneously, we must all write to the same manufacturer on the same night.

In other words, we will write *en masse* to Ford on Monday night, to Fiat Tuesday night, Volvo on Wednesday night. Then, in order to save the makers of my own new car till last, we will all of us send off a letter to Renault Thursday night.

That way, you see, when Friday comes –

It'll be 'All write Honda' night.

'Rose of Washington Square'

Song, 1920: Words by Ballard MacDonald
Music by James F. Hanley
Also title of musical film starring Alice Faye

THE worst part of any match or conflict is the waiting. The actual coming-to-grips with the opposition is hot-blooded and exciting but the period beforehand is dreaded by everybody.

And when the conflict is an international needle match which will decide whether England will be back in Europe, the morale of the lads is of paramount importance if the result is not to be a defeat or a draw.

So you can well imagine that early in the morning of October the twenty-first, Horatio Nelson was a very worried admiral indeed.

His flagship, *HMS Victory*, and a couple of dozen English warships and some supply vessels were hove to, wallowing in the swell of Cape Trafalgar at the foot of the Spanish peninsular, waiting for Napoleon's fleet to come out of Cádiz and make a run for the Mediterranean. They had been waiting for days now and boredom hung heavy over the entire fleet.

In the great aft cabin of *HMS Victory* Nelson was slumped over the breakfast table, idly modelling shapes in the butter.

Nelson's personal steward Able-Seaman Falcon (like most stewards in the British Navy he was Maltese) stopped leaning against the wall and ambled over to see what Nelson had fashioned.

'They're Lady Hamilton's bosoms!' he said.

'How do you know?' said Nelson, looking up sharply.

The steward was saved by the distant sound of drunken singing wafting in through the open windows.

'Well, somebody's happy!' said the steward. He looked out. 'It's those Britishers who hire sailing boats at Portsmouth so they can follow us and watch the battles. They've spent all night boozing in the Cádiz bars by the sound of 'em!'

'Lugger louts!' said Nelson, flattening Lady Hamilton's bust with the back of a large dessert spoon.

'Sir,' said the steward, after an hour or so. 'Call me a fool if you will – '

'You're a Maltese fool,' said Nelson. He was bent over the table modelling other memorable bits of Lady Hamilton in the butter.

'No, not *yet*,' said the steward. 'Hear what I say first, m'lord. I think you should do something about the men. The battle might start any moment now so there might not be much time. You know the Fleet has got a sweepstake on when the first shot will be fired, well I've picked later on this morning, 11.40 am to be exact (he was dead right, won first prize of £28,560 and after the battle became a landowner and MP, with a stately home near Brize Norton). The morale of the lads is very, very low, sir admiral milord. Couldn't you think of something to cheer 'em up?'

'Like a poetry recital?'

The steward closed his eyes for a moment. 'That *sort* of thing, sir. Though I was thinking along the lines of who can drink the most rum before exploding. Something entertaining like that.'

Nelson detached Lady Hamilton from his thumb and lightly buttered a ship's biscuit with her bottom. 'Yeeeeees,' he said thoughtfully, chewing. 'You're absolutely right. What the chaps *really* need, of course, is a stimulating appeal to their patriotism – that always gets 'em going – a stirring appeal to their sense of duty from the whole nation – got a pen?'

He scribbled busily on the tablecloth. 'I intend to send this signal to the entire fleet. "Your country, as Shakespeare put it, this sceptr'd isle, set in a silver sea, hopes that with a bit of luck . . ."'

'A mite longish, sir, if I might make so bold. How about "England expects . . ."'

'Good. "England expects that every manjack of you of whatever race, colour creed, religious persuasion, size of boot, colour of hair . . ."'

'I would make it just a little bit briefer, sir, or the signal flags won't be able to cope. How about "England expects that every man . . ."'

'Excellent. ". . . that every man, when the battle begins as indicated by the bosun on his whistle, will pursue his particular task as detailed by his section officer without leaving his post or putting in for compassionate leave though shot and shell may rage and it comes on to rain or he feels bit off-colour . . ."'

22

'How about simply ". . . will do his duty?"'

'". . . will do his duty."' Nelson looked down at the tablecloth on which the signal was written, visibly moved. 'It is quite the most glorious and stately signal I have ever composed, Falcon,' he said, a vagrant tear rolling down one cheek (one cheek only for obvious reasons). 'It will ring round the world and end up strung across the Maritime Museum. Send for the Signals Officer.'

Captain Hardy arrived. 'Duty Signals Officer and Ship's Captain reporting, milord,' he said, saluting rather beautifully.

'Be so good as to break out the signal flags and fly this signal for the entire fleet – nay the whole world – to read.' cried Lord Nelson, whipping off the tablecloth with a grand gesture and handing it to Hardy.

'Ah,' said Hardy. 'Snag is, milord, we have a wee problemette. We haven't *got* any signal flags. We *had* signal flags. But we have no signal flags now.'

'But how can you not have signal flags, Hardy? You are the Signals Officer. What on earth is the point of having a Signals Officer who isn't able to signal?'

'It doesn't necessarily follow,' said Hardy, cautiously. 'You can have a Vice-Admiral who is happily married and goes to church.'

'Hardy, out with it, man, what have you done with our signal flags?'

'I lent them to the Mayor of Portsmouth, sir. For his Parish Church Grand Fête. His bunting was all torn so I lent him our signal flags to use as bunting. According to the Mayor somebody very holy stole the lot.'

Nelson was breathing heavily. 'It is a keel hauling offence to set sail without signal flags. You're for it, Hardy, unless you can produce a set of usable signal flags pretty damn chop-chop.'

Hardy stumbled to the rear window of the cabin, his mind racing. Looking out, he noticed that wallowing behind the *Victory* was a tiny, ancient supply vessel with a stout woman scrubbing the deck.

'Avast behind!' he hailed.

She turned her head round. 'What of it, cocky?' she shouted back.

'I am Captain Hardy, you common person. Your skipper has a set of signal-flags. Send them over immediately in a longboat. Or a shortboat if that's all you've got, the matter is too urgent for me to stand on ceremony.'

The woman went below and told the captain who groaned miserably. He had had enough trouble on this voyage already. Starting with the woman, who came on board in Portsmouth to do the ship's laundry as per custom but fell asleep and sailed with the ship as a reluctant stowaway. The captain, a shy bachelor, did not quite know what to do with her so he signed her on and just off Cape Finnisterre she became his First Mate.

But worse than that, before sailing from Portsmouth the Mayor had persuaded the captain to lend him the ship's set of signal flags to replace his fête's worn bunting and later the Mayor apologised and said that somebody had stolen the signal flags (the captain wondered later why the Mayor needed to borrow signal flags anyway as he happened to know that the Mayor made his living selling them secondhand.)

Then the captain remembered that sailing one of His Majesty's ships without signal flags was punishable by keel-hauling. 'Oh, deary me!' he moaned, rocking from side to side. 'Oh, crickey, poor old me!'

'What's up, ducky?' cried his First Mate, cuddling his head, for she had turned out to be salt of the earth.

He explained. 'What's a signal flag look like, then, ducky?' she asked him. He said that it was a square piece of highly-coloured cotton. Each flag was a different colour in a different shape and each meant something in the code-book.

'Right,' said the broad-hipped paragon. 'Fetch me those baskets of laundry, which I never got round to ironing.' And with her powerful fingers she tore the crew's multi-coloured shirts, curtains and duvet-covers into square pieces, choosing each piece to match one of the flags in the *Master Mariner's Code Book of Signals*.

Half an hour later the captain rowed the pieces of coloured cloth over to the *Victory* in his ship's wideboat. A few minutes later the signal was hoisted proudly up to the topyards of the *Victory* and the whole fleet cheered as they spelled out, flag by flag, the most famous naval signal ever: 'England Expects That Every Man Will Do His Duty'.

But you and I know that it was not official Admiralty signal flags which displayed the historic message. It was something much homelier:

Rows of washing, torn square.

For whom the bell tolls

Sermon by John Donne
Title of Hemingway novel

ON THE sixteenth of last month, at exactly 7.47 in the morning, my diet died. Prior to that, I had been going in for various methods of losing weight almost continuously for nearly three decades, which means that over the whole period I must have lost something like six hundred and seventy two pounds; the equivalent of about three Nigel Lawsons or eight Ronnie Corbetts. On the pure mathematics of it, I should now have been able to hang from a charm bracelet.

It doesn't seem to work that way, though, which goes some way towards explaining why I called a halt. 'Enough is enough,' I finally said to myself, and anyone else within earshot of the bathroom scales. 'My body may not be much, but it's been jolly good company all these years, so why go on punishing it? The time has come to tear up the diet sheets and cease being a slave to will-power and cottage cheese. From now on, it's farewell to the push-ups and the exercise bicycle and the local (or Lo-Cal) Health Club. Henceforth, the only thing I shall exercise is my right not to exercise.'

Let me fill in the background to the decision. As with so many people, after my physique had weathered a fistful of decades, it started to develop what I can only describe as an immunity to being thin. Obviously, I took all possible steps to counter this tendency but after battling with it for several years without success, I found myself entertaining certain doubts. Might not Nature have visited this new configuration upon me because, in her wisdom, she knew thinness was no longer in my best interests?

Once started upon that thought, I found it more and more attractive. After all, doesn't it seem entirely fitting that the same destiny that shapes our ends should also end our shapes? Convinced

25

I had hit upon a truth vouchsafed to few, I took the big step. On the date mentioned earlier, I shredded my Weight Watchers membership card and resigned myself to what Kenneth Tynan called 'the lateral fusion of waist and hip'.

Although life certainly became more relaxed once I had settled for becoming avocado shaped, it did have a few disadvantages. Chief among them was the discovery that the only things in my wardrobe that didn't have to be exchanged for a size larger were my scarf and umbrella. Not an unreasonable price to pay, I thought, till I found it involved saying farewell to my two favourite items of apparel – a couple of crocodile leather belts I had bought at a ridiculously low price in Ibiza, back in the days when the pound was still worth nearly seven shillings.

The prospect of losing the use of those two belts simply because the holes at present punched in them would soon be insufficient to accomodate my waistline was almost too much to bear. I was seriously contemplating going back on the yoghurts and crispbreads when, unexpectedly, a possible solution to the problem arrived in the post. It was an invitation to a small private dinner at a luxurious hotel in Park Lane.

'In what wise can that be considered a solution?' those of you who use the 'in that wise' construction will be demanding. Well, merely posing the question reveals that you can never have even tried to drill fresh holes in an old leather belt. The one thing anyone who has had the most perfunctory go at it will have learned is that there is no finer tool for the task than a kebab skewer. And where are the strongest and sharpest kebab skewers to be found? In the kitchens of any establishment that is Arab owned! (Now do you see why I was so excited to discover it was a *Park Lane* hotel?)

Consequently the first thing I did on arriving there was to hand the magnificently uniformed doorman my two belts, with the request that he convey them to the Head Chef with my compliments and would the Head Chef please be so kind as to pierce both of them carefully with one of his excellent kebab skewers at the places indicated by pencilled crosses.

Looking back now, it would probably have been wiser if I'd gone along to the kitchen myself and explained what was needed. One sees with the benefit of hindsight that if a non-English speaking maître de cuisine is presented with any kind of out of the ordinary request, he is going to take it as an indication of the way somebody wants something cooked. Never mind that the something in question appears to be a pair of crocodile leather belts – this hotel, you must remember, is one which positively boasts about the unorthodox culinary demands made on it by its international clientele. Chef probably shrugged it off as nowhere near as bizarre as the things he gets asked to cook on Burns Night.

In the event, there were two things about the meal I am never likely to forget. The first was the expression on the faces of my fellow diners when the polished dome of a silver serving dish was raised to reveal two gently steaming leather belts nestling on a bed of lettuce.

The second was the question asked by the waiter as he proffered the dish to the assembled company. With only slightly elevated eyebrows, he enquired –

For whom the belt-holes?

Popocatepetl

A volcano in Mexico

I HAVE at last perceived a use for cats.

Freud (Siggy, not Sir Clem) once confessed that the answer to one question had eluded him throughout his distinguished life. The question was 'What do women *want*?' A similarly difficult question the old boy might well have pondered was 'What is the point of cats?'

A French poet once wrote (and I translate): 'A cat are the Good God's methodical to allow or permit a human hand to caress a tiger.' Now this is patently rubbish so I looked up the poet: his surname was Méri, but his christian names were the giveaway; he had four of them: François – Joseph – Pierre – Agnès. I put it to you that there is simply no taking the word of a nineteenth-century French poet who has three male Christian names and one female which together sound like a Belgian pop group on the Eurovision Song Contest. The point is that stroking a cat is nothing whatsoever like caressing a tiger. I have never actually, myself personally, put palm to tiger as my arm is about thirty feet too short for comfort but at the London Zoo I have drawn my hand along the back of a cheetah, a beast of much the same make. And I do not recommend it. My palm came away scored with blood-red stripes as though I had been at it vigorously with one of those wire-brushes used by the Navy to de-rust battleships. To pretend that you can emulate this experience by stroking a cat is – if I might break fluently into Monsieur Méri's own tongue – *stupide*.

So if to be a surrogate tiger is not the purpose of cats, what is? Might their function be to astound mankind with their feline intelligence? It might not, I humbly submit, if you watch them at work and play.

28

In my view, and I have a cat or two in my view most hours of the day, your average mog may be a feline computer of finely-tuned instincts but in the matter of intelligence is as thick as a Sumo wrestler's groin. A cat is a dab hand at bringing you in half a mouse in the middle of the night in case you feel in need of a snack but terrified of going through the cat door, which it has negotiated safely a couple of thousand times, in case there is a purple monster waiting on the other side.

On the other hand, are cats on this earth, do you suppose, to demonstrate affection? To teach humans how to love one another. I deeply hope not.

Our younger cat, Cinto, an Abyssinian, is full of affection and sometimes his need for showing me how much he loves me is so great that he waits until I am unsuspecting and then takes a running jump from about thirty feet away on to the back of my neck. And he is not a small cat. His face is quite small but he gets bigger behind, like a Boeing 747 which has a tiny cockpit but becomes a barrack-block as you move towards the tail. That amount of loving cat crashing into the back of one's neck is quite an experience, particularly if one is doing one's toenails at the time or sipping a cup of hot coffee.

Kettering, our Burmese cat, is now an old gentleman. He, too, loves me with a love which has to be expressed. Kettering expresses it mid-morning when I am working and oblivious to everything but how rotten the prose is on the typewriter. He slides into the study unseen, collects himself behind me, rocks a few times to get the distance right and then launches himself into the air to land deftly on my shoulder. At least, that is the general idea. The trouble is that Ketters is not as lithe as he used to be, nor as good at judging distance. The result is that he either sails right over me and crash-lands onto the typewriter, mewing piteously, or he jumps low and starts sliding down the back of my jersey. This frightens him, so, understandably, he unsheaths his claws and digs in. His claws, which are like those hooks which dockers used to use for heaving heavy sacks about, go through my jersey, shirt and a quarter of an inch of flesh and he hangs there. I cannot reach him. I have to go down the drive to the brick pillar of the gate, back up to it so that Ketters is more or less sitting on top of the pillar, and then bend at the knees in the manner of Dixon of Dock Green saying 'Evenin' all!' It might take several attempts, by which time a small crowd has usually collected, but eventually I can manage to unhook him and carry him back to his basket.

Mighty hunters! Greatly daring! Is it the function of cats to remind humans of the ancient hunting skills which the human race had forgotten? Oh, surely not. What sort of mighty hunter cannot locate its supper unless you ram its nose into the saucer?

When there is a cold chicken in the fridge our two hunters go into a B-movie robbery routine. Cinto is the stake-out man. He sits in front of the fridge and gazes at it unblinkingly for hours. He is willing the fridge door to swing open. He will stay for days if we do not eat the chicken.

Once the pair of them decide in their miniscule brains that despite their hopes the door is not going to melt, nor the cold chicken leap out and surrender, Ketters, the peter-man gets down to it. He works away at the bottom edge of the door with a gently probing claw. Sometimes the door is not properly shut, usually because of something like a litre bottle of a Chianti-style red wine-substitute being too fat for the rack, and Ketters can swing the door wide open. Squeaking slightly with excitement, the robbers stand on their hind legs and pull the cold chicken out and it lands with a wet thud on to the floor in front of them.

Then what happens?

The two Great Thinkers have not the faintest idea what to do with a whole, cold chicken. It is suddenly unfriendly. It looms over them, chilly, alien, the wrong colour and shape for real food which always come in nice little brown lumps from a tin. So they affect indifference. They sit down and blink slowly several times. Then they stroll off.

It was while I was watching them work the fridge caper that I noticed a curious thing. It was the clue I needed to establish once and for all what the real use of cats is.

The proper function of cats is to assist those human beings with bad colds to choose roses.

The curious thing which I noticed was that when the cats were burgling the fridge they sniffed at all sorts of food on the shelves and turned away immediately from anything which had a nice smell. Yet they were quite happy to play with something quite odourless like a Bath Oliver biscuit or a slice of supermarket processed cheddar. Further scientific tests confirmed my observation: I offered our cats a saucer of decent sherry and they were not the slightest bit interested. In fact they turned away with a *moue* of distaste. The same happened with a pounded-up clove of garlic, a curiously-strong peppermint and a banana. My theory held.

Do you see now the practical application of my discovery, how you can put your cat's one natural aptitude to practical use?

Then I'll tell you. When your wife asks you to call in to the Garden Centre and bring home some old-fashioned cabbage roses with strong scents (as mine once did), and you have a heavy cold and could not smell a skunk blasting off eight inches away from your nose (as I once had), and you do not want to admit to the cold or you would not be allowed to go out on Saturday evening (as I also wanted to do), this is what you do: you go to the Garden Centre and make a note of all the cabbage roses which look as though they might be scented. You then steal a small blossom from each and label it.

Although *you* cannot smell anything and do not know whether a blossom is scented or not, your cats know and will play happily with the unscented ones and leave the scented ones untouched.

So when you get home all you have to do is call your moggies to you, take out the labelled blossoms, and from each blossom in turn –

Pop a cat a petal.

IT REALLY is beginning to look as though I can be talked into writing anything, provided the money is right. Nothing else could explain my current assignment, an attempt to turn an ancient Eskimo folk epic into a peak time mini-series for Channel 4.

Admittedly, its story-line is quite compelling, if only because you so rarely come across a romantic tragedy that takes place in a temperature of forty degrees below. (Come to think of it, there's probably not that many romantic triumphs, either.) But the other thing the plot has going for it is its hero, a young Eskimo whose whole life is dedicated to his harpoon. With good reason, I should add – so responsive is it to his hand, he has become the most successful walrus hunter in the entire Arctic, rejoicing in many furs, a luxury igloo and a top-of-the-range sledge whose features include an extra husky at the back for reverse.

Nevertheless, it is a bleak kind of existence, especially as his only living relatives are the two elderly aunts who have looked after him ever since his parents perished in a penguin stampede. Nowadays, unfortunately, it is he who has to look after them, one of the consequences of an acrimonious incident when both ladies tried to climb into the hole in his kayak at the same time. As a result, each of them now has only one eye and they spend their days squatting on separate ice-floes arguing about who should have had precedence.

But our young hunter is still very fond of them and they remain the only feminine influence in his life till the day he happens to fall over a young Eskimo girl who has been lying face downward in a snowdrift to help clear up her complexion. When his clumsy attempts at rubbing off the snowshoe marks he has imprinted on her parka are greeted with unexpected appreciativeness, he proposes they meet next day in some more interesting mound of snow. And, inevitably – because encounters with unattached females in this part of the world are about as rare as bananas – before the next solstice rolls around they are married.

It is after she becomes his wife that the story takes a strange and sinister turn. Suddenly, almost overnight, the young man's mastery of his harpoon seems to desert him. No matter how carefully he aims the weapon which hitherto has served him so faithfully, the sharpened end now invariably lands somewhere other than intended.

At no time is this more distressingly illustrated than the afternoon he launches it at a group of basking walruses. Clambering across the tundra to retrieve his prey, he is horrified to find that what the harpoon has skewered is no walrus – it is one of his beloved monocular aunts! (Stationed, as was her habit, on an adjacent ice-floe, she had by the sheerest bad luck been squatting with her good eye scanning the wrong horizon.)

Beside himself with grief, the young man tries to administer nose to nose resuscitation. When that fails he swears a mighty oath – never again will he use his faithless harpoon, even if it means giving up hunting altogether and existing for the rest of his life on frozen foods.

It is a vow to which he adheres rigorously until, some months later, his wife returns from the local medicine man with the news that they will soon be hearing the chatter of tiny teeth. If they are to clothe the new arrival, she announces, to say nothing of building an extension on the igloo, he will simply have to go out and replenish the fur supply.

So, heavy at heart, he retrieves the harpoon from its ceremonial burial place and once more ventures forth. This time, though, he takes care to keep to the sunniest part of the ice where, after only a short prowl, he espies a sight to gladden any Eskimo heart. There, within easy range, sits a large polar bear, fanning itself with a small seal. Taking a deep breath, the young hunter balances his harpoon in the palm of his hand, then – aiming with consummate care – he lets fly.

When he hears a muffled grunt from an ice-floe to the left of the polar bear, he can scarcely bring himself to look – and when he does so, his worst fears are confirmed. The small squatting figure into which the harpoon embedded itself is his sole remaining one-eyed aunt.

A great cry escapes from the young man. Half demented with guilt and grief, he tries to commit suicide by throwing himself in the path of an advancing glacier. Abandoning the attempt only when he realises it is one of those that move forward at a rate of two metres per decade, he rushes home and, grabbing his wife, shatters his harpoon into a hundred pieces over her head.

Although it is a gesture that many scholars consider one of the most eloquent moments of renunciation in all Eskimo drama, that is not how his wife perceives it. 'What you picking on me for?' she asks. 'What have I done?'

'I don't know what you've done,' he screams back. 'I only know that before you came on the scene, that harpoon of mine would hit anything I aimed it at. Now, though . . .' – and here he unconsciously anticipates an old Irving Berlin tune –

'It only harpoons one-eyed aunts with you.'

An ill favoured thing, sir, but mine own

William Shakespeare
'As You Like It' Act Four, Scene four.

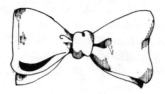

I REMEMBER so well piping out this line in my childish tenor on the stage of Leyton County High School for Boys. I piped it out to the Headmaster, Dr Quiller-Couch (old Q's nephew, as it happens). The occasion was not the school play but the judging of an inter-school culinary competition.

I was aged thirteen and I had at the time, but not now, a wooden leg. I'll come to that later, or I might not. It depends on my mood as the story progresses.

Leyton County High School for Boys was a fine educational establishment the like of which no longer exists, or if it does it is called something like 'The Essex Education Sub-Committee's Citizen's Workshop PLC, for Post-Puberty Customers'. It is not to be confused with Leyton County High School for Girls which was in Leytonstone and was our bitterest rival in such games as boys could decently play with girls. We were in fact very frightened of girls and when beside them on the touchline at mixed hockey matches would exert our superiority by punching them repeatedly on the upper arm.

What provoked the whole incident was a programme on the wireless (no telly of any consequence in those days. Only a few sets like filing cabinets with screens the size of a Jacob's Cream Cracker, and according to the BBC's research department, watched solely by a few dozen wireless dealers and – inexplicably – the late Queen Mary). This wireless programme was moaning about the lack of interest in good food in Britain and it blamed schools for not teaching schoolgirls how to squeeze the goodness out of a kilo of *truffles* and get that extra touch of bizazz into their *bisque d'homard*.

The programme also banged on about boys being utterly useless in the kitchen, being messy and taking much too long over everything.

The programme coincided with a trip some of us boys took to the LCHS for Girls to join in a mixed lecture on 'Space – Whither?', to be followed by lunch cooked, for an exam, by the girls of Lower Third Cookery and Housewhiffery.

The exam lunch the girls gave us consisted of fingers of damp, dead quiche, fried liver (a thin purse of horsehide which, when cut into, oozed sawdust), and stewed apple (with the toe-nails left in).

When Dr Couch heard our report on the meal he was incensed. 'We must show them that even boys entirely untutored in culinary arts can do better than *that*!' he said, banging a fist into his palm so hard that his mortar-board slid sideways. Although he usually resembled Seneca, for a moment he looked exactly like Will Hay.

And so he devised and announced his Inter-School Cookery Contest, LCHS for Boys v. LCHS for Girls. One girl and one boy were to be elected and on Saturday morning at ten o'clock in the school hall, with both schools watching, a sealed envelope would be opened revealing the dish which was to be prepared. The contestants would be given two shillings and sixpence each to buy the ingredients and would have exactly one hour and a half to go away and prepare the dish. The tasting would take place at exactly twelve o'clock, midday.

The judges were the Headmaster, the Headmistress and one of the governors of our school, a retired Canon who always, even in midsummer, had a dewdrop on the end of his nose. The rules stated firmly that if either contestant was late in with his or her dish or had accepted help from friends or a mummy, he or she would be disqualified.

I was elected to represent the LCHS for Boys, never having cooked even a tin of baked beans in my life. The representative of the LCHS for Girls was a senior girl called Marie-Claire who had lots of dark hair, a cross on a chain round her neck and was such an odd shape above the waist that it occured to me that she might find it quite difficult to go in for serious rowing or playing the piano accordion.

At half-past ten, the Canon opened the secret envelope and read out the news we had been waiting for. The dish Marie-Claire and I had to compete over was – Trifle! My favourite food! 'Go!' cried the Headmaster, banging a bell.

36

Off we shot. Unfortunately I had a disability. My wooden leg. I was going to play Long John Silver in the Public Library Play-Reading Group's production of *Treasure Island* and I was working in my wooden leg, which was my normal leg bent at the knee and strapped up, with a sink plunger attached to the knee with insulating tape.

It was not too uncomfortble but it made the bike ride home to make the trifle a complicated matter. The wooden end of the sink plunger would not fit happily on the metal 'rat-trap' pedal. In fact it did not fit on it at all. Every time I tried to push on that pedal the wooden leg sent the pedal spinning and the leg carried on down until it hit the road which sandpapered a quarter of an inch off the end of it.

So I had to get off and push the bike. By the time arrived home I was horrified to find that, allowing time to get back to the school by twelve, I had only about eight minutes to make the trifle. And another point sprang to mind. How does one make a trifle?

I sat down, rested my wooden leg on the dog and tried frantically to remember what a trifle consisted of. Well, there had to be – sponge fingers! Raced (hopped, actually) to the kitchen and the cupboard under the sink. There, in a bucket, were the floor cloths and – a sponge. Cut the sponge into fingers and put them in a glass bowl.

Next? Quickly. Custard! I remembered it began as a tin of yellow powder. No tins of yellow powder in kitchen cupboards. Found a tin of talcum powder and poured some over sponge fingers, adding a large spoonful of Colmans mustard powder to give it the yellow look. Shoved the bowl under the tap and whisked up the mixture. Looked good.

Trifles had to have red jam. Back to the kitchen cupboards. Gooseberry jam. Honey. Lemon curd (that takes you back a bit). Nothing red. Except, at the back of the cupboard with the fuse wire and hammer, a tin of red paint. Poured it generously over the trifle. Dipped finger in and tasted. Not bad at all; a remote, melancholy taste, like the water from dead daffodils.

On! On! Only a few minutes left. What is missing? Think! The trifle is almost finished but one vital ingredient is still missing . . . of course! Jelly!

I hopped round to Leyton street market and round the stalls.

They sold old prams, second-hand fishing rods, sandpaper, but not one of them sold jelly. But there was one stall selling jellied eels.

I still had my half-crown intact and in those days you could buy a surprising amount of jellied eels for half a crown. I walked away with a huge cardboard tub full of the stuff. I picked out the bits of eel and gave them to a stray dog who became very grateful and stayed with me. In fact he stayed with me for eleven years and eventually died of old age. I stirred up the remaining jelly with my comb and jiggled it over the trifle. I had done it!

Pooh, it stank! A terrible smell of bad ocean, like the bottom of Southend pier at low tide; a sour, salty, rancid offence to the nostrils.

Half-hopping, half riding the bike on one pedal like a scooter, I rushed back to the school. As I climbed on to the platform the clock said eleven fifty-nine.

There was no sign of my rival, Marie-Claire. The girls were twittering with worry. The boys were confidently purring.

'Sir,' I said to the Headmaster, handing him the bowl. 'Here is my trifle.'

He took a tentative, chef-like sniff and reeled back. The scent from my bowl also wafted across to the Headmistress who went 'Yuuuuuoink!' and sought a handkerchief.

The school clock struck twelve.

'The smell!' said the Headmaster. 'Muir, what in God's name *is* this?'

In my piping schoolboy voice I claimed victory:

'An eel-flavoured thing, sir, but by noon.'

'I'm Dancing With Tears In My Eyes'

Old popular song

SOME years ago, a literary weekly posed the question, 'Which opening phrase would be most likely to deter you from reading what follows?' The one deemed most unpromising turned out to be 'If, as seems unlikely' – and, to my profound regret, never once since have I found myself with a legitimate reason to start a piece with those words. Till now.

If, as seems unlikely, I am ever invited to write one of those 'Disaster Movies', I know exactly what I would base it on. My adolescence. You see, at the age of fourteen – I was six-foot-two.

Have you any idea what a painful experience it is to enter the difficult years of puberty at that altitude? I found it so excruciatingly embarrassing, I would never even tell people what my measurements were. Whenever anybody enquired how tall I was, I would mutter, 'Five foot fourteen.'

Matters were not improved by the fact that I was skinny with it. All sticking-out wrist-bones, twig-like ankles, elbows you could slice cheese with and no shoulders at all till I reached seventeen. (Even then, I'm told, I only had one.)

But height was my big problem. I admit that, in the normal way of things, being taller than everyone around you can have certain advantages: you can look down blouses; during a drought, any rainfall reaches you a millisecond or so earlier. But at age fourteen, all it makes you feel is conspicuous. I would estimate that from that year till the day I became seventeen – and thus could, as they say, 'carry it' – the physical activity I most frequently indulged in was crouching.

But there is something else that must be remembered about the fourteen-year-old male. He is at an age when all that hormonal stuff starts happening. And, in my case, that was what led to the most distressing aspect of the vertical disparity between me and everybody else in my peer group.

I found that girls were unwilling to dance with me. To appreciate what a serious deprivation that was, you must remember that we are dealing with an era when the only opportunity a growing lad had for a close encounter of any kind was at the Palais. Dancing in those days was still very much a contact sport – you didn't so much dance *with* a girl as *among* her – and popular mythology had it that even those licenced conjunctions could be surpassed if you obeyed certain recommended techniques while dancing.

One of these was to keep your gaze steadfastly locked to your partner's throughout the dance. It made steering a bit erratic, but it apparently kept a girl's attention from straying to whatever the mysterious things were that girls usually thought about. However, the other attention-getter was the one the best authorities considered so surefire, that, it would leave absolutely any girl in the same state of quivering eagerness they habitually left you in. This was the one known as 'dancing cheek-to-cheek'.

Could I now prevail on you to employ the hemisphere of your brain which summons up visual images? There was I, six-foot-two – and that year the average height favoured by the girls of Stamford Hill was not a gnat's eyelash above five-foot three. If we deal with the 'holding the gaze' technique first, the only way any girl that size could manage an eyeball-to-eyeball dance with me was by assuming the posture used by spectators at the Farnborough Air Show. After two girls fell over backwards, I gave up the whole idea.

I was more reluctant to abandon the cheek-to-cheek technique. Apart from its acknowledged potency, I'd overheard certain blonde girls explain that the main reason they preferred not to dance with me was because my superior elevation permitted me to look down on their dark roots. With my cheek at the level of theirs, that danger could be avoided.

But how can six-foot two possibly go cheek-to-cheek with five-foot three? In the event, I only managed it by curling myself round and downwards into the shape of a sort of round-shouldered question mark. After two or three weeks of this, my back was giving me such gyp – I still have to see a man in Wimpole Street about it every few months – I settled for what might be described as a kind of halfway cheek-to-cheek. In other words, my partner and I retained the 'pressed closely together' aspect, but we both remained upright. I suppose you could call in 'cheek-to-chest'.

It might well have worked, too, had it not been for another characteristic that year's crop of Stamford Hill girls shared – an inordinate devotion to those chunky, spiky ear-rings popularised by Betty Grable.

Again, I must make a call on your visual imagination. Try and picture what happens when a girl who has been dancing with her head pressed to a chap's chest unknowingly gets one of her chunky, spiky ear-rings pronged into his knitted tie. Does it not become plain that when the music stops, and she pulls away – a small bit of ear-lobe will remain?

It was my small but rapidly growing collection of ear-lobe fragments that finally persuaded me to give up the Palais and seek heartsease elsewhere. I can recall to this day the horrified revulsion with which, as I surveyed my assortment of blood-stained neckwear, I heard myself murmuring –

'I'm dancing with ears in my ties.'

'Your Eyes are the Eyes of a Woman in Love'

Words and Music: Frank Loesser
Sung in the film version of 'Guys and Dolls'

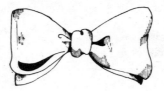

WHEN the Thorpe Players Amateur Dramatic
Society (Hon. President and co-Founder F. Muir) reached its
thirtieth birthday, the members decided to celebrate by staging an
ambitious musical-comedy. It was the time that the National
Theatre had put on a stunning production of *Guys and Dolls* and
thus legitimised musical shows as perfectly respectable fodder for
serious amateur societies, whose idea of a frivolous birthday production up to then had been to do *King Lear* in seventeenth-century
dress.

Fired by the enthusiasm of the Thorpe Players, I promised to
write them a musical comedy. Not a show based upon a short story
as was *Guys and Dolls* but a wholly original concept, a treat for the
ear and the eye devised, created, conceived and written by me.

I am going to call it *Guy and Doll*.

A wonderful title, you must admit, which came to me out of
nowhere one night in bed as I lay sleepless after two helpings of
take-away Mexican lasagne in a cheese and onion sauce.

The Guy in question is an English naval officer on secret service
in France during the Napoleonic Wars. His full name is Lieutenant
Guy Woode-Wynde. Woode-Wynde is a somewhat quieter version
of his uncle, who is the British Admiral, Hornblower. The Doll
whom Guy falls in love with at the end of Act One is Doll Duvet, a
continental version of Shakespeare's Doll Tearsheet, that is to say
plumper and warmer.

The plot – which will be laid down in Act One, scene one, in a
dialogue between Admiral Hornblower and his comical bo'sun – is
that the British navy is beseiging the port of Le Havre in order to
make it surrender. Horrific tales are coming out of Le Havre of the

shortage of food and the French inhabitants starving and being forced to eat things like shepherd's pie and high-fibre muesli.

But Hornblower is cautious. Before attacking Le Havre he sends a signal to his young nephew ashore, Guy the Spy, saying 'How hungry is Le Havre? Please reply as briefly as possible as the Admiralty is cutting down on expensive signals and I have now only a small allowance per war. And I would be most grateful if, in your travels, you could get hold of some of that Normandy cheese that I like, not the kind wrapped in leaves but the sort which has the picture of a grinning cow on the label. Your aunt's leg is better and she is thinking of getting rid of her chrysanthemums – such a bore the rest of the year – and going flat out on azaleas. I counselled caution but she is so headstrong, God bless her little secateurs. Well, cheerio for now and don't do anything I wouldn't do, ha-ha! Uncle Horatio.'

Scene two is set in the Latin quarter of Le Havre (red lights are shining over squalid doorways reeking of vice. And, of course, over dentists). Guy enters disguised as a non-combatant, an American on the Grand Tour. (You can tell because he wears tartan cotton trousers and looks exasperated.) From out of a doorway marked 'Sailors' Mission' comes a huge, beautiful young woman.

'Oiiiiiiii!' she bellows in a lovely voice which carries over most of sleepy Le Havre. 'Oiiiiiiii! All you young sailor boys! Come and get eet! I got 'ere what you want, eh? Oiiiiiiiiiiiiiiiii! Ze mission she is open for ze night – all night!'

It is Doll Duvet, chucker-in at the Sailors' Rest Mission. The disguised Guy, duty bound, enters the Mission to see what supplies they have managed to get past the English naval blockade. Do they buy food from foreign sailors? Guy casually asks Doll whether the Mission is open to sailors of all nations.

'Oui,' says Dol, 'Always we got plenny Scandinavians.' And she goes into the show's first musical number:

> 'I gotta Norse right here,
> The name is Paul Revere . . .'

Guy realises that he is fascinated by every aspect of this enormous lady, from her fine chins to her petite, beclogged feet. He feels he might be falling in love with her but if so would it be a case of too much, too early?

On impulse he offers her a lump of the cheese with the grinning cow on the label which his uncle Horatio asked him to get.

'Zat processed muck!' said Doll bridling. 'Zank you, non! You see, my charming friend – I 'ave my pride.'

'Mother's Pride?' cried Guy. Here was potential trouble. It meant that the siege was being broken by unscrupulous English supermarkets floating their cut and wrapped loaves across the channel.

'Non,' said Doll. 'I do not like ze English plastic foam. I like ze French country bread. Like a crisp, golden cow-pat. And when you guillotine it into slices ze bits of crust ricochet off the walls like bullets. Listen, mon ami – ' she lowers her voice into a whisper. 'Demain – tomorrow – ma tante, she smuggle me a fresh loaf baked in ze communal oven in ze poor but proud leetle village of Verneuille-des-trois-églises-entre-les-deux-lacs-en-haut-de-Bûgey-sur-Epiney.'

'But surely,' Guy mumbles, 'Chewing a piece of grinning cow cheese now won't do you any harm?'

'Patience, dearest,' says Doll, taking his tiny hand in her vast fist and looking deeply into his eyes, 'Leave us not rush destiny.'

And she begins to sing her second number:

'I'll gnaw when my loaf comes along . . .'

While she is singing, Guy writes out his dispatch with his other hand, reporting that the Le Havre populace is coping well in spite of a worrying lack of stewing steak and glacé cherries for the gin-and-Its.

As Doll finishes her song there is a disturbance. Three Chinese seamen have set fire to a small chair and are balancing on the flames a domed metal dish. All three are busily cutting up a riding-boot and stirring the pieces of leather about in the bowl.

Guy realises that he must get away from this temptress or he will forever rest a captive in the fiefdom of her heart.

'My love, you have not eaten,' cries Doll. 'Dinner will be served soon.'

'Must go!' cries Guy, thickly, leaping to his feet.

'No, you mustn't!' cries Doll, pointing dramatically to the Chinese and breaking into her third song, a lively spiritual:

'Sit down, they're wok-ing the boot . . .'

The action gets v. exciting at this point. A messenger rushes in to announce that Nelson has won the battle of Trafalgar Square, a signal is flying above the square which reads 'England expects that every man will do his washing' and the War is over. There is dancing and singing in the streets. Guy and Doll are separated. Guy stumbles around trying to find Doll in the crowds of revellers but only hears her in the distance calling to him: '*Oiiiii! Oiiiiiiiiiiiiii!*'

The last act shows Guy twenty years later, now stinking rich, having won the concession to import French cheese with a picture of a grinning cow on it into Britain. He has hardly ever married, just a couple or so times, because his heart has always belonged to Doll.

At the age of sixty he decides to make one last effort to find his Doll and books himself a voyage round the world in a balloon left over from a Jules Verne story. A grand ceremony is planned in Portsmouth for the balloon's take-off. The Mayor of Portsmouth has decorated the balloon with signal flags which he has rented out to Guy for a large sum of money. But a sudden sea-mist descends and take-off is postponed until the morning.

Guy wanders into town to while away the evening. He is strolling through the port area, the mist getting thicker and swirling round him, when he hears in the distance 'Oiiiii, Oiiiiiii'. 'Tis my Doll!' he cries, sprinting in the direction of the beloved voice. He falls into the water quite a few times but as he gets closer to her the cry gets louder and louder until – '*Oiiiiiiiiiii! Oiiiiiiiiiiiiii!*' – and there she is, a massive silhouette in the mist.

'Doll!' he cries, clasping her to him and slipping a ring upon her finger.

'But, cher Guy, it is dark – and the mist – you can't see – how do you *know* it is me after all these years?'

And the show ends on the big waltz number, this time sung by Guy. 'How do I *know* it is you?' cries Guy, leading her down to the footlights. 'Because, my dear . . .'

'Your *Oiiiiiiiiii*s are the *Oiiiiiiiiii*s of a woman in Le Havre . . .'

Do not count your chickens
until they are hatched

Proverb

Y OU have asked for a tale of the French Revolu-
tion, m'sieu, so it is to that turbulent period of our history I will
address myself.

Let us, then, return ourselves to the year 1792, when Marie
Antoinette's indifference to the sensibilities of the C and D sectors
in French society was summed up by a recommendation which even
to this day has the power to sicken the stomach: 'Let them eat
quiche'. As a consequence, it was not long before the downtrodden
and the underdogs of la belle France rose up to pit themselves
against the uptrodden and the overdogs.

Within the space of two short years – owing to Louis XVI's gross
mishandling of the economy, most years were short at that time –
the monarchy was overthrown, a dictatorship of the Committee of
Public Safety was established, and so much aristocratic blood was
shed, the cobbles in front of the guillotine were stained bright blue.

One of your English poets was kind enough to observe, 'Bliss was
it in that dawn to be alive' – and, as we now know from other
contemporary sources, even half-alive was good. Because although
the Revolution set brother against brother – a spectacle only to be
seen nowadays in certain episodes of *Dallas* – it also provided
instances of gallantry rarely encountered since, before, after or
during.

And perhaps the most inspiring of those was the conduct of one
of France's most distinguished noblemen, Le Comte Phillipe De
Tour. Up till now, he had escaped the attentions of Danton and his
infamous Committee because of the high respect he enjoyed as the
most eminent road builder in all Europe. In fact, even in Great
Britain, you will still frequently see the name De Tour displayed on

46

busy traffic highways. (It is one of the ironies of history that, by contrast, the word 'Danton' now survives only as the title of a chart-topping record by Petula Clark.)

But to return to the period whereof I speak, it was a time when the Committee were in a mood of some anxiety. According to a survey they had recently conducted, the number of people coming to the Palace de Grève every Saturday morning to watch the regular eleven o'clock guillotinings had significantly decreased. This left the Committee facing a difficult question – how could they win those viewers back?

Throughout history, whenever those responsible for mass entertainment have been confronted with the problem of falling audience figures, they have always proposed the same solution: 'Give them bigger names!' So it proved with Danton. He immediately commissioned another questionnaire, this time asking 2000 typical guillotine-goers which of the surviving aristos would they most like to see ascend the scaffold?

When ninety-two per cent of the respondents named the Count De Tour, it became obvious that any previous immunity was no longer to be relied upon. Within days, the Count was dragged before the tribunal, which lost no time in sentencing him to the same fate as his aristocratic friends – or, as the lower orders called them, pedigree chums.

However, as Frenchmen never tire of telling you, fortune is a fickle jade, *mon ami*. What Danton and his underlings had neglected to take into account was that mysterious factor I mentioned earlier, 'gallantry'. For, as anyone who knew him would have confirmed, De Tour was a man in whom an unusual degree of courage was allied to that equally crowd-pleasing attribute known as 'style'. Not for nothing had an English milord of his acquaintance given him the affectionate nickname of 'Jereboam' – a nomenclature of no significance to the Gallic ear but, I am assured, cherished by the British as indicating 'a lot of bottle'.

There was no doubting its presence on the morning they required him to appear at the Place de Grève. Not only was he the only aristo since the fall of the Bastille to toss the driver of the tumbril a substantial tip, but his last words to the guillotine operator were 'Thank you for not smoking.'

It was behaviour that won a round of spontaneous applause from every onlooker present, even the gnarled old women who sat at the

47

foot of the scaffold knitting fishnet stockings for what would later become the Folies Bergères. Its effects on the mood of the rest of the populace were startling. When the Committee came to take its next Opinion Poll, the results showed a swing of no less than four point five per cent *against* the Revolution.

It was a shift in public support so dramatic, Danton was obliged to furnish his guillotine personnel with an edict which some scholars consider as historically significant as the one that came out at Nantes but got revoked. 'For the greater good of our glorious Revolution,' it began, 'You will henceforth not place any member of the higher aristocracy under the blade until he has shown himself to be totally incapable of manifesting any form of personal courage.'

Or, if m'sieu would prefer me to put that edict in more colloquial language –

'Do not hatchet your counts until they are chicken.'

'Tales from the Vienna Woods'

Johann Strauss the Second

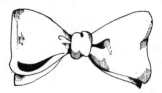

M Y LADY wife and I were humming this Strauss waltz only this morning in celebration of a small victory we have achieved over the forces of change, with the help of a modern high-tech product and a new shop in Virginia Water's shopping parade (the superior end).

My wife and I have lived in the same house now for thirty-five years. For some reason this news astonishes citizens much more than the fact that we have been married to each other for forty years.

Quite frequently in summer, when taking a refreshing glass of mid-morning champagne on the lawn – we can't afford French mineral water – we see heads rising above our fence and dropping back. They are usually the heads of middle-aged couples who have driven down from places like Gnosall, Staffordshire, or Towcester, with a small exercise trampoline each in the boot of the car. They place these on the pavement outside our house and then bounce on them higher and higher until they can see over our fence. 'They have lived here for thirty-five years!' they exclaim to each other at the height of their bounce, sometimes audibly when the wind is in the south-east, and then drop down out of sight. We occasionally hear the trampolines being pushed back into the boot of the car and the car being restarted for the long journey home.

The reason why we have stayed in this house so long is that we like it. We liked it from the moment we saw it and we have continued liking it ever since because we have not made changes to it. Mrs Muir and I do not like change.

This is the story of how this idyllic state of affairs very nearly went terribly wrong a few weeks ago. It is a story which is extremely short of laughs but is, I think, interesting. Or, failing that, semi-interesting.

It was something our son said when he came down for a weekend visit. It was one of those oblique comments which we took no notice of at the time but which later set us worrying. We turned over and over in our minds what he said. Was he trying to *tell* us something?

His actual words were, 'You've let this house become a slum. You must do something about it or it'll be condemned.'

Eventually it was Mrs Muir who twigged what he was getting at. He was suggesting to us that we had let Anners (which is the name of the house) get a little behind the times and that we should bring its appurtenanaces and decor more up to date.

The scales dropped from our eyes (I have never understood that expression. What were the scales doing there in the first place? Was the expression first used in reference to fish? Or pianists? I don't see the point). We walked round the house looking at it in a new light and making jottings on a small pad.

The first thing we noted for consideration was the difficulty of opening our front door, which for strangers is baffling. The other day the phone rang while a visitor was here and our kindly visitor immediately rose and said 'Don't worry, it's time I went – I'll see myself out.' The telephone call was then rendered inaudible by bangs, squeals, crashes and fearful oaths coming from the direction of the front door. Vicar just couldn't get the door open. But Mrs Muir and I had a conference and decided it was basically the visitor's fault.

It should be obvious to anybody that to open our front door from the inside, you stand with your right side hard up against the door, grasp the door-handle firmly with your right hand and lift it with all your strength a quarter of an inch. At the same time you brace the side of your right foot against the bottom of the door, pull *inwards* on the handle and strike the top, non-hinge corner of the door a fierce blow with the clenched fist of your left hand. The front door then opens effortlessly. There is absoluteluy no need for us to change the door, it seems to us.

And then there's the downstairs loo. It is the same story. User ineptitude. No reason for us to change it. Mrs Muir and I have no trouble at all with the thing although it is sixty years old. All you need to do is grip the dangling handle on the end of the chain and gently pull – *gently* pull – accelerating smoothly for three inches.

Then you must pause. The pause is absolutely vital. Then, as if catching it unawares, you tug the handle quite viciously for an inch and finish on a smooth *diminuendo*.

The trouble is with guests that they will snatch. Then the lever hits the bottom of the tank with a horrid metallic 'clonk'. I cannot remember how many times we have heard that dread 'clonk' coming from the downstairs loo after a guest has excused herself and left the room and either Mrs Muir or I have had to slip away to her rescue, a matter of kneeling at the loo keyhole and talking her, as it were, down. We always spoke in a disguised voice to avoid any embarrassment when she returned to the drawing-room (I usually adopted the tones of a jovial New Zealander, Mrs Muir 'those of a Castilian duenna). It is then simply a matter of 'Don't snatch at the chain, madam. Gently – gently, does it – now again – *gently* and pause – NOW PULL! – not quite – begin again – easy – easy – PAUSE – PULL! Oh, well done!'

But it was when we applied our new eyes to the kitchen that we realised that our son's strictures could not be ignored and we had a problem.

It had been the farmhouse scullery and the walls were gradually shrugging off a hundred years of old wallpaper. The most recent wallpaper (thirty-five years old) was hanging off the walls in festoons (for years I had noticed that something tickled the back of my neck when I was bent over my breakfast egg but I thought nothing of it). Beneath that was a rather pretty paper of a floral design – rather like pink cauliflowers – now much faded and stained with rising damp, with here and there a live mushroom doing rather well. That paper had rotted away from parts of the wall to reveal a much older paper with a jolly sporting scene beneath, ladies in ankle-length dresses, wasp waists and huge straw boaters waving egg-shaped tennis racquets. Beneath *that* paper were glimpses of lath and cow-dung wall with the odd silverfish making a furtive journey across it.

Yes, the kitchen was a beautiful sight, enough to gladden the eye of all who, like us, love the old-world, unsophisticated way of life. But there was no doubt that it was also a health hazard. 'Tiles!' we both said dully, at the same time, with despair in our voices.

So off we went to nearby Virginia Water to buy horrible, hygienic tiles, of some frightful modern design no doubt, to cover the loveliness of our kitchen walls.

But it was not quite like that. A new and exciting interior

decorating shop has opened in the parade (there is always one shop in every parade which seems to change hands every six weeks. This one had been a Home Security shop selling alarms and things but it got burgled. It was then a Serbo-Croat Takeaway but when the customers saw the Serbo-Croat Takeaway food they left it where it was on the counter and the place was closed under the Trade Descriptions Act). The sign above the shop now reads: 'The Hon. F. Ward and Husband: Decor for the Daring'. Inside was a thin lady with black lipstick and a see-through blouse with nothing through there to see, as it were. 'I'm the Honourable Fiona!' she said to us. 'What fun! That's my husband, Mr Ward!' pointing at a small, bearded, bloodless man skulking in the corner. 'Tiles! They've gone heavenly! Let me tell you about this fantastical new range!'

The Hon. Fiona and Mr Ward had discovered a German firm which made up tiles by a photographic process which converted a beloved snapshot into a complete wall.

'Mrs Muir!' I exclaimed in mounting excitement. 'Modern technology has come to our rescue! I will photograph each kitchen wall and get these delightful people to have the snaps turned into wall tiles! We will then still live in our old beloved kitchen but we will be able to hose it down annually!'

Shortly after the photographic tiles were put up they were put to the test. Jim Knight and his lovely wife Nora, who have the fish shop up at Virginia Water, came to deliver a prawn (Mrs Muir was making a prawn curry and was a prawn short so Jim and Nora brought it down in their refrigerated van. Say what you like about small traders but you get service).

'What a marvellous old farmhouse kitchen,' said Nora, bearing the prawn on a salver. 'Yes, and still the same old wall paper!' exclaimed Jim.

'Not quite!' said I, springing forward and sloshing tomato sauce all over it.

'Have you gone doo-lally?' cried Jim, starting forward.

'Not quite!' said I. 'Watch!' And whipping my shirt tails out of my trousers I rubbed the wall clean in a trice.

'Crumbs!' said Jim. 'If it is not wallpaper, which it clearly isn't, what in heaven's name is covering those walls?'

I answered, with a half-concealed smile of triumph,

'Tiles from the Fiona Wards'.

'An American in Paris'

Gershwin tone poem and title of film

WHEN I was in Form Five at Craven Mount School, we were reckoned to be what would probably now be called 'The A Team'. Today, surveying the crowd at our first Reunion Tea Party, I found myself reflecting that that was going on for forty years ago; could it really be true that the only one who didn't appear to have changed very much was me?

And, it would seem – her. Once again, my eyes strayed to the willowy and elegant figure at the far end of the room. Of all my former classmates, she was the only one I could not put a name to.

Take Penny Williefield, for instance. I had spotted her the moment I came in because, despite the years, she looked exactly the same from the back. The fact that it turned out to be her front made no difference to the warmth with which we greeted each other and exchanged histories. Dear sexy Penny, whose father's allotment-shed had been known to every red-blooded Form Fiver as 'The OK Corral'. Nowadays she was a giggly size sixteen who, as she lost no time in telling me, had been only too happy to settle down and breed Sealyhams. She didn't offer much information about her husband, Sir Charles Sealyham, but I gathered he was something fairly distinguished with a Who's Who nearly nine inches long.

As Penny moved away, my eyes returned to the mystery woman. She was still standing by herself, but any hint of aloofness was dispelled by the unmistakeable mischief in her smile as she surveyed our fellow guests. While I was trying to decide whether to move over to her, somebody slapped me on the shoulder.

'Hallo, oldtimer. You tell me how great I'm looking, then I'll lie to you.'

Would this be Ginger Anderson? Thanks to the fact that when red-headed men go bald they go a redder shade of baldness than other bald men go, I was able to assure myself that this was indeed him. Or 'he', as Mr Murchison would have insisted we say.

Dear old Murchy – now there was someone I'd have been willing to bandy reminiscences about with old Ginge for hours. He'd been our English teacher, a man so committed to the glories of English prose, he once made Fire Drill a written test. Ginger, however, had never been one of his favourites – 'Because I objected to his making us go to the loo in alphabetical order' – so we set about recalling some of the other notable members of the teaching staff: old Mrs Huxtable, who'd brought disgrace on the school by sending in a forged request to 'Family Favourites'; young Miss O'Gorman, who would chalk an algebra problem on the top bit of the blackboard while simultaneously rubbing out whatever was chalked on the middle bit.

But what of the pupils they had tended during those long-ago years? What had they made of themselves since? Ginger, who had always been the class gossip, was only to pleased to supply potted biographies.

'See Les Conroy over there – remember how he found Geometry so difficult, he never did learn how to calculate the shortest distance between two points? He's now running a highly successful fleet of mini-cabs. And Stan Tozer, in that corner, chatting to Priscilla Ollerenshaw – 'member how he was so dead certain he was going to be famous one day, every time we had a school photograph taken, he used to hold a sign saying "This is me", so as to make it easier for his biographers? Told me his present line of work is assistant bingo caller. And Herbie Lovelock there – you can't have forgotten how he lost his position as Hall Monitor the afternoon he tried to strip-search the netball team. Funny how things work out. These days he owns that big mail-order company, Club Smut.'

Fascinating as it was to discover the strange turns the lives of my friends had taken, my thoughts kept returning to that coolly provocative figure across the room. Without drawing Ginger's attention to her, I tried to discover which of Form Five's former temptresses she might be. Irene Livermore perhaps?

'Old Reen? A right neurotic that one, wasn't she? Remember when you wouldn't let her have a lend of your Captain Of The Clouds Decoder Ring, so she drank her young brother's chemistry set? Straightened herself out though, and last I heard she was

Economics Correspondent for *Honey* magazine. Pity she couldn't get here today, I liked old Reen.'

'What about Alice Pacefoot – she here?'

'Always fancied her, didn't you. No, she couldn't get away either, because she's now got this job as a paid informer. Works on the Information Desk at Heathrow.'

So which of my former classmates could the mystery lady be? As Ginger slipped off to refresh his drink, I closed my eyes and mentally ran through the class register. Halfway through the L's, I suddenly started getting that crawly kind of feeling that means an unseen somebody is staring at you. On opening my eyes I discovered who the somebody was.

As she watched me make my way through the crowd towards her, the smile on her face was the kind I would have described as teasing – an impression heightened by her first words. 'You haven't got the faintest idea who I am, have you?'

I shook my head. 'You must have changed more than anybody here.'

'That may well be true,' she said. Then – 'I'm Anna Murray.'

My mind fast-forwarded through that class-register again. 'We didn't have an Anna Murray,' I said. 'There was an Edward Murray . . .'

'That's me,' she said. 'Edward Murray. As was.'

As I tried to explain to Ginger when he came across to find out why my complexion had suddenly gone the colour of shrimp cocktail, the trouble about going to reunions these days is that there are now so many ways they can wreak emotional havoc on you. Not only do you find that somebody like Stan Tozer can arouse pity, or Herbie Lovelock provoke scorn, but – to paraphrase a Gene Kelly film –

'Anna Murray can embarrass.'

A Room With a View

Title of novel by E. M. Forster

I N THOSE far distant days when I was a school-
boy it was the sentimental ambition of most of my classmates to
grow up as quickly as possible and move out of home into a Room
with a View. A Room, that is to say, that did not have to match up
to parents' obsessive standards of hygiene, and with A View, a far
as the boy was concerned, to persuading a girl to share the room
with him (to satisfy a young male's most urgent need – somebody to
look after him).

I was the first of my gang to manage it; to achieve E. M. Forster's
title, or something which sounds quite like it if you read it out aloud
and quickly.

At that time of my life, when I was twelve and a half years old
and ageing rapidly, I was a boy in whom ambition burned with a
gem-like flame. Not *worthy* ambition like becoming a missionary or
growing up clean in thought, word and deed, or being Britain's
Ambassador to the political powder-keg which men called Mesopotamia (what happened to Mesopotamia? Is it still where it was,
wherever that was? You don't read much about it these days.
Package tours seem to give it a miss, which is a pointer). My
ambitions, which I pursued with the ferocity of a mating tiger
rounding on David Attenborough, were in retrospect verging on the
trivial.

Growing up is much a matter of being stimulated by visual images
and having the senses woken, which is why an afternoon visit to the
Bohemia Cinema, High Street, Broadstairs (seats ninepence, and
one and three, or in through the EXIT door in the alley which did
not close properly) in Spring, 1932, and an hour and a half of
Ramon Navarro playing Armand, the elegant, suave lounge lizard

in *She Who Dared* was enough for me to set my sights on becoming likewise and cutting a swathe through the married ladies of East Kent.

It was an ambition doomed to failure from the start. Armand had a tiny, pencilled moustache such as it was beyond my capability to grow. In those days one could buy clip-on moustaches for use in amateur theatricals and I tried to wear one of those but the effect was not right. The moustache was much too bushy (my model was called the 'Old Bill') and the slightest breath of wind sent it dipping and bucking, which made the wire clip up my nose extremely painful.

Also there was the matter of clothes. Armand wore an overcoat with a fur collar slung carelessly over his shoulders. I bought a rabbit-skin from our butcher and glued it to the collar of my raincoat and slung it round my shoulders. It was not perfect, but looking at myself in the hall mirror I detected a whiff of the urbane scoundrel. But it came to nothing. I had to run for the school bus and my fur-tipped raincoat fell off and was trodden on by a horse.

Then I read in a magazine about college youths in America who demonstrated their devil-may-care courage by outdoing each other in foolhardy pranks, like stealing a light aircraft and putting it through aerobatics or staging a running race along the top of the New York to Chicago express train. Instant ambition flared up within me. I would go one better. But which one? The answer came in a moment of inspiration. On Broadstairs pier, where there was no traffic, I would mount my bicycle. (Raleigh, Sturmey-Archer three-speed) and pedal for a count of twenty seconds WITH MY EYES SHUT!

Think of the nerve required. Can he do it or will he crack and peek? was in everybody's mind as my friends from Form Four A foregathered sombrely on the pier at the appointed time. My bicycle was checked for ASDIC devices. Witnesses were posted along the pier to watch that my eyes were tightly closed.

At the sound of 'GO!' I screwed up my eyes – and my courage – and set off, pedalling as fast as I could so that I would keep a straight course. I heard the umpire's voice through the megaphone, fading as I left him behind, 'Nine seconds . . . ten seconds . . . eleven seconds . . .'

I might have made it but on the count of seventeen I ran out of pier.

57

It was not until I was nudging my thirteenth birthday that my luck changed and I, at last, achieved my ambition – and gloriously.

I had run through quite a few ambitions since being fished out of the sea off the pier. There was the period when I desperately wanted to be able to touch the end of my nose with my tongue. Curious how it seemed so important to me then and how much less it matters to me these days; I have hardly attempted it for weeks now.

The breakthrough came unexpectedly. A distant relation – he lived in London – took me to see a car race at Brooklands. I was enraptured. All the senses were seduced. The glorious sweeping Brooklands track, soaring up in curved banking, was simply beautiful.

And then there were the totally new sounds and smells. As the great Bentleys and Lagondas and Bugattis fought with each other round the track, the ear was filled with the mechanical equivalent of jungle roars: RRRROOOOOOMM-BRRM-RRROOOOOOMMM!

And hanging in the air above everything was the exotic, sweet/sour, somehow middle-eastern smell of hot castor oil.

Back at Broadstairs I set to with feverish dedication. My ambition, now an obsession, was to sit at the wheel of a Brooklands racing machine, making that roaring, savage sound as I accelerated and changed gear, all the while enveloped in the pungent pong of hot castor oil.

I swapped my five shilling Ingersoll pocket watch with Prescott A. (Form Upper 3B) for his no longer used pedal-car, constructed to resemble an Alpha-Romeo by his father, a chartered accountant. It was difficult to pedal because of my height, but I could just manage by splaying my knees out of the cockpit like chickens' wings and pedalling with the sides of my feet.

To achieve the essential noise I tried taping a bit of cardboard so that it stuck through the spokes of the front wheel but the cardboard wore out in a few yards. So I borrowed a celluloid collar from the vicar of the Congregational Church, cut out an L-shaped piece of celluloid, drilled a hole in the middle and a hole at the end of the arm and fixed it to the car's front mudguard with a bolt, threaded a piece of string through the hole in the arm so that when I pulled the string it worked like a bell-lever and the culluloid was pushed into the spokes of the wheel.

It worked like a dream; the noise was *exactly* like a racing-car on the go.

Next came the problem of creating the authentic smell. I bought a small bottle of castor oil from the chemist. How to make it hot. When you are a boy growing up in a seaside town like Broadstairs you prospect every evening on the beach to pick up what holiday makers have dropped out of their rolled-up towels or their pockets. I found exactly what I needed. A lacy kind of garment like a very short vest. It had shoulder-straps and was split into two pockets which were clearly meant to hold shoulder-blades. I went on to the rocky end of the beach and found two large pebbles which more or less fitted into the two pockets.

On the great day I pedalled my car to the recreation ground which had an oval running-track. There I got a small bonfire going and heated my two large stones. I dragged them out of the fire, wrapped them in cotton wool and placed them carefully in the pockets of the lacy vest, put the vest on and, holding the bottle of castor oil over my right shoulder, poured the lot over the hot stones.

The smell was incredibly authentic. It WAS Brooklands.

Exulting, I bent over the pedals and hurtled round the oval track, operating my celluloid strip of vicar's collar to produce the growling roar when I accelerated and leaving an odour of pungent hot castor oil hanging heavily in the air behind me.

I had achieved my ambition:

A RRROOOOOOOOOOM – with a *Pheeew*.

Cutting off one's nose to spite one's face

Proverb

WHAT is it that drives a man to keep his underpants in the freezer? I cannot answer for the mass of humanity, but in my case it was August Strindberg, the tormented Swedish dramatist responsible for such powerful works as *Miss Julie* and *The Dance of Death*.

For those to whom the connection may not be immediately apparent, let me explain that I have recently been working on a hitherto undiscovered Strindberg manuscript, believed to be the only bedroom farce he ever wrote. That makes it not only a theatrical find of surpassing cultural signficance, but also – to quote the producer who commissioned me for the task – a stone bonk certainty for a summer season at Blackpool this year, especially if I can work in references to Prince Charles, Michael Jackson and the toffee-nosed neighbouring resort of Lytham St Annes. It would also take the heat off him no end, the producer said, if I could introduce a walk-on part for his research assistant, a black-satin skirted lady with what appeared to be an inner-sprung blouse.

The only other specification he considered worth mentioning was that my fee for the job was contingent on the completed script arriving on his desk by first thing Friday morning. Otherwise, forget it.

As this was the Monday, that gave me just under four days. And it soon became apparent that I was going to have a bit of trouble meeting that deadline. Not, I hasten to say, because of any problem inherent in the text. On the contrary; immaculate craftsman that he was, Strindberg had made sure that it was absolutely loaded with laughs and smut. No, the difficulty turned out to be my sleeping habits.

I don't know whether I've ever mentioned my lifelong insomnia to you. Probably not, because I don't make a big thing about it. As far as I'm concerned insomnia is no more than Nature's way of letting people know what the ceiling looks like at three in the morning – but there is a certain paradox about it which is probably only familiar to fellow-insomniacs. It is this: people who find it difficult to fall asleep at night find it equally difficult *not* to fall asleep the following afternoon.

Well, like most other sufferers, I eventually found a way of adjusting to that biological inconsistency. I have simply got into the habit of taking a refreshing twenty-minute nap every day straight after I finish lunch. I admit it sometimes makes the staff at Macdonalds a wee bit tetchy, but aren't the Italians always telling us that regular cat-naps are what prolong a man's life? (Unless, I suppose, he's at the wheel of a Fiat.)

However, when that four-day Strindberg commitment came my way, there was no time for an after-lunch crash-out. On the other hand, if a body has become used to a daily twenty minutes of surcease, when it is suddenly deprived of it, withdrawal symptoms set in. Round about two-thirty pm, the eyelids start growing heavy, the breathing becomes slower, and the legs sag towards stuffed upholstery. It is the call of the kip.

So my collaboration with Strindberg resolved itself into a problem of what might be called 'resisting a rest'. To maintain productivity, I somehow had to counter my inbuilt snooze button.

Reason told me that what I needed was some form of early warning system, an alarm device that could be set off by the very first onset of a zizz. Could that be achieved, I wondered, by wearing an electrified tie? The detailed circuitry eluded me, but what I pictured was that the instant the tie felt my chin droop down on it, it would respond by delivering a small but powerful electric shock that would immediately jolt my head upwards again. The idea might well have been a practicable one, but it's something I did not get an opportunity to find out, because when I got on to the Electricity people about wiring me up, they said they wouldn't be able to send a man round for at least another eight weeks.

The local furniture showroom proved no more helpful when I went in to enquire whether they might be able to make me a specially designed wake-up chair. What I had in mind was one which, when it sensed the weight of its occupant beginning to slump slowly downwards, could somehow be triggered into hurling his whole body to the floor. When the salesmen leant closer and confided that most of the chairs they sold seemed to do that anyway, I thought it best to try another tack.

My son has always been a dab hand with gadgetry, so I asked him whether he had any ideas as to how I might restore my post-lunchtime energy level. After brooding on the problem, he hit on a solution which I suppose would have met the technical requirements, but (A), it was not one hundred per cent foolproof, and (B), those jump-leads did my ear-lobes no good at all.

In the end, it was a book that led me to the idea of ice-cold underpants. Rummaging through the library shelves, I came across a piece of research proving that sleep could be most effectively kept at bay by what it called 'cold extremities'. After giving considerable thought to the question of which extremity was likely to be the best one for that purpose, I began my daily practice of stepping into a pair of freezer-fresh underpants immediately after lunch.

And it worked. Well, let me qualify that slightly. While there is absolutely no doubt that they can dispel the slightest flicker of incipient sleepiness, icy underpants are not really the most *helpful* things to wear while writing a sexy bedroom farce.

By the same token, though, they did lead me to an interesting variation on a more proverbial exercise in self-denial –

Cutting off one's snooze to speed one's farce.

'I Wonder Who's Kissing Her Now'

Words: Will M. Hough and Frank R. Adams
Music: Joseph E. Howard and Harold Orlob

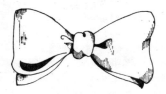

FROM THE DESK OF MR FRANK MUIR Esq
Senior Chairman
'SETALIGHT' GLOBAL TELEVISION PRODUCTIONS
GROUP INC. LTD.
Fax No. Pending.

Suite 1A, c/o Stanley Alwyn's Hairdressing Salon
The basement, 110 Shaftesbury Avenue.
London W1
Tel: Temporarily disconnected but hopefully will be reconnected
by Thursday.

ANNOUNCING an INVESTMENT opportunity in my new block-buster so-called soap opera which is going into immediate production as soon as possible.

This is now YOUR chance to INVEST NOW in a SURE-FIRE HIT and make millions at least.

MORE GLITZIER, more SEXIER, more BETTERER IN EVERY WAY than anything in which Joan Collins has been in or similar and a dead cert for satellite showing (satellite telly will get version B with topless jacuzzi scenes) with subsequent enormous profits for all and sundry.

Here, to send you stampeding for your cheque book, is, free and *au gratin*, a resumé of the plot.

THE PLOT

The soap (as we in the trade call it) tells the continuing story of a poor girl born in Brooklyn, America, who grows up lovely yet

63

nurtures within her bosom (which with a bit of luck you will get a glimpse of in the satellite version if the actress concerned does not object or ask for more money) three lusts. Her lusts are: (1) to be famous, (2) to be powerful, and (3) to be rich. Not just ordinary rich like you and me will become when the series is sold but rich as the proverbial Creosote.

Her mummy and daddy are poor Latvian refugees named Carl and Beulah Loof (hopefully to be played by Kirk Douglas and Cher). They call their pretty little daughter Wanda, so her full name is Wanda Loof. Unlike her parents she is, of course, American bred. This gives her all the ambitions and opportunities which the denizens of the United States have always achieved and dreamed of ever since their new and vibrant nation was discovered and plunged into the melting pot.

Wanda grows up a gorgeously beautiful redhead, brunette or blonde (according to who we can afford) girl, fun-loving and at one and the same time highly intelligent as well. In fact at Brooklyn University she majors in Classical Drama and Modern Tap and minors in Psychology.

But within her the three ambitions burn and she sets about making her first come true – to become famous. This she decides to do by making undoubted use of her talents as an actress by becoming a Hollywood film star.

She gets a job as a cocktail waitress in a famous Hollywood restaurant where all the film producers go. It is called *Nero's Place* and she is required to wear a toga with an extremely low neckline. Howard Hughes the famous producer is sitting there one day. She bends low before him to serve him his Diocletian Double Daquiri. Howard Hughes looks up, sees, gulps, and realises he has found the new curvaceous star he needs for his big picture, *The Inlaw*, the powerful story of a cowboy and his young and beautiful mother-in-law. Wanda is to play the Inlaw and Hughes shows her on the posters lying back voluptuously on a heap of hay under the slogan, 'Mean, Moody, Magnanimous'. He marries her to save paying her a salary and the picture is a huge success. Wanda achieves fame throughout the world.

AMBITION NUMBER TWO – TO BE POWERFUL: Now famous, Wanda divorces Howard Hughes who immediately becomes a recluse and vanishes. Wanda goes to where all the powerful people congregate – Washington. She lies under the sun at friends' swimming pools all day and pops up at important people's parties in the evenings golden-brown – the toast of Washington.

Washington's most powerful politician, Henry Kissinger, falls madly in love with her and proposes marriage. They have a huge society wedding where their wedding march is sung by Frank Sinatra (I hope to get Des O'Connor, who is interested). They are happy for two or three months and then Wanda realises that power brings with it heartache. Life as the wife of such a powerful man as Henry Kissinger is tiring her out. She is on her mettle every time she appears in public and she begins to exhibit signs of mettle-fatigue. So she decides to divorce Henry Kissinger and fulfil her third and last ambition.

AMBITION NUMBER THREE – TO BE EXTREMELY RICH: Wanda divorces Henry Kissinger and moves to Wall Street determined to make her fortune. There she hears about Charles Dow, a brilliant financial journalist who has what a girl seeks in a husband, and sackfuls of the stuff.

Charles Dow, with a friend, Mr Jones, publishes a newspaper all about money called the *Wall Street Journal* which has made both of them very rich indeed. They have also invented a column which daily points a finger at which stocks and shares are going to drop in value like stones. This column, which is reprinted all over the world, is called 'The Dow-Jones Index Finger'.

Wanda accidentally meets Charles Dow one day when he is taking his day's profits to the bank in a convoy. He is laughing all the way. Wanda loves laughter so she laughs with him and he invites her to sit with him in the leading tank and help him count the $100 notes, removing those which are grubby or crumpled. Wanda has never been so happy. Chuckling like a child, she screws up all the $100 banknotes which are not brand new and tosses them playfully in the direction of her handbag. Dow, who is a baseball fan, is impressed by how this ravishing beauty never once misses the handbag and falls in love with her. They marry. In three months he turns the marriage settlements she received from Mr Hughes and Mr Kissinger into an enormous fortune and makes Wanda the wealthiest woman East of Elizabeth Taylor.

The title shot will be Wanda sitting smiling in her Park Avenue mansion symbolically cuddling a sweet little white poodle who has a million dollars worth of diamonds sewn on to its collar and lead (every soap has to have a rich bitch in it).

All that is left is to name our super, superb show. It has to be an egotistical title, like the series about the famous Roman Emperor, *I, Claudius* or the story about the famous rugby-football player, *I, Zingari*. But, as American divorcees like Wanda tend to hang on to their ex-husbands' surnames and preserve them in the middle of their current name, our title comes out a bit longer. Our award-winning dramatic soap-opera is proudly entitled:

I, WANDA HUGHES KISSINGER DOW

Can I get there by candle-light?

From the nursery rhyme, 'How many miles to Babylon?'

I COULD have begun this tale with either my failed 1960s business venture or the unhappy experience I had at Cricklewood Broadway, but I decided it might be less confusing if I started with an observation on the subject of hoarding. In the whole field of human relationships, there exists no source of conflict more bitter than that between people who can't bear to throw things away and people who can.

As one who belongs to the first group, permit me to offer heartfelt greetings to those of you out there who also fall into that category. As the Rodgers and Hammerstein song puts it, 'Hello, Junk Lovers, Wherever You Are.'

Except, of course, 'junk' is a word that would only ever be heard on the lips of the other lot: the 'non-hoarders' of this world. Non-hoarders, as I hardly need to remind my bunch, are the people who are forever waylaying you with questions like, 'What is the point of hanging on to a full set of 1957 telephone directories?' Or, 'Do you realise we now have enough old Christmas bows and decorative paper to wrap up Birmingham?' Or, 'Just tell me why you insist on keeping that old mirror with no glass in it? Are you expecting it to *heal*?'

What they do not understand, those persons who can *part with* stuff, is that some of us who lived through the rationing and shortages of World War Two have been left pathologically unable to throw anything away. Why else would I still stubbornly cling on to broken drill-bits, bent nails, and half a folding ruler? An elderly clock that only works when you lay it face-downwards? Umpteen Lifetime Guarantees for products whose manufacturers went out of business round about the time of Suez?

As for the little wads of cotton-wool you find at the top of aspirin bottles, I now have enough of them to stuff a duvet. (To say nothing of all the empty aspirin bottles.)

I would not for a moment deny that this stockpiling of what some might term inessentials does arouse hostility among the other member of the household. She is likely to meet you at the front door with such implied reproaches as, 'Know how many black plastic bags I've just filled with your cruddy rubbish? Eighteen! And there still isn't one drawer in the house that closes all the way!' (Incidentally; any of you fellow-hoarders noticed how the things you find yourself reluctant to relinquish are cruddy rubbish, while hers are 'precious mementos'?) 'Just tell me,' she asks 'What conceivable *use* is all that stuff?'

It serves absolutely no purpose to try and explain that the concept of 'use' is quite irrelevant to this particular idiosyncracy. If we hoarders only hoarded things 'because they may come in useful', why do I find myself looking for an empty shoebox in which to store the little bits of rope that are left when the soap has been finished in a Soap On A Rope?

No, the pursuit of that line of argument gets you nowhere. A lifetime of hoarding has taught me that there is only one successful way of placating the inflamed emotions it seems to provoke. You have to demonstrate that although you cannot give up the inclination, you will at least make an effort to keep the accumulated chattels in some sort of order. That is why, last year, I announced I would henceforth keep a detailed inventory of them.

And I was as good as my word. Well, almost. I bought one of those enormous, Dickensian ledgers and began using it to enter details of every item I had placed up in our loft. And out in our garage. And in our spare room. And underneath our stairs. And inside our car-boot. And beneath our bed.

The process became so fascinating that I still recall every word of the first two entries I made. *Item One* described an object left over from an enterprise I was involved in during the sixties. At that time, the whole world flocked to what was then known as Swinging London, and among the most popular of the items bought by visitors to Carnaby Street was an apparently empty can, containing what the label promised was 'Authentic London Air'.

I, of course, was in my usual fortunate position of having quite a stock of empty cans – over seven hundred, the other member of the household estimated – so I took a couple of gross of them from their storage place in my son's spare cot, and drove them to the top of Highgate Hill, where the London air is reputed to be cleanest. Once up there, I removed each one's lid with my right hand, fanned some breeze into it with the left, and put the lid back on again. I then rushed all of them to my man in Carnaby Street, who pasted our own privately printed labels on them.

Regrettably, the venture left me quite a bit out of pocket. I never really understood why, but my Carnaby Street partner assured me it was due to a combination of the American dollar being against us and the Soviet wheat crop failing. He was, however, good enough to sell me back one of the cans to keep as a souvenir and that, as I say became *Item One*.

Item Two was more straightforward. That went back to the beginning of 1972, when I made a New Year's resolution to cycle to the office every day. Knowing this would mean leaving home while it was dark, I fixed a specially powerful lamp on the handlebars and on Jan. 3rd I set out for the first time.

Unfortunately, what I had neglected to take into account was how much earlier than usual I had to get up, with the result that while I was waiting for the lights to change at Cricklewood Broadway, I fell asleep. The bicycle was a write-off, but the lamp survived to become the second item in the inventory.

I wish I could tell you about some of the other colourful and interesting keepsakes I catalogued, but I'm afraid those two proved to be the only ones. After entering them, I went to look for somewhere to store the massive ledger and found there was no space for it anywhere in the house.

So that is my other tip to my brother (and sister) hoarders. Do allow yourself that little bit of room for your inventory, otherwise you may wind up with a list of items so brief that – in my case, at least – it almost takes on the appearance of a nursery rhyme . . .

Can, Highgate air,
Bike-handle light

Onward Christian Soldiers

Hymn

IF I LIVE to be a hundred, which wouldn't take all that long, I will never be allowed to forget the names of those lads who shared a Nissen hut with me at RAF Station, Kaldadarnes, Iceland, in the winter of 1942.

There were just six of them. On the surface just ordinary aircraftsmen of no particular distinction, one an engine fitter, another a cook, another a clerk and so on, but when crisis faced our hut, they welded together into as devious and corrupt a gang of thieves dedicated to self-preservation as any man could wish to have about him.

The crisis came when winter arrived and our hut at night was as cosy as a hole in a glacier. The airfield at Kaldadarnes was being built by the Pioneer Corps but was as yet unfinished. There were trenches around our hut dug and waiting to be filled with concrete for foundations. These filled with water during the day and froze over at night so sleep, if any came, was constantly disturbed by sudden sharp shrieks as revellers staggering back from a few pints in the NAAFI fell through the ice.

In December, 1942, it was cold enough at Kaldadarnes to freeze the bails off a set of brass cricket stumps. We had no beds to lie on and gusts of icy wind came up through the gaps in the floor boards like razor blades.

Leading Aircraftsman Joss Nankeville called a meeting to discuss the emergency. Joss was the brains of our hut, a natural leader. Somebody heard an officer say that Joss was head boy at Lancing so we thought he was a vet but then we realised that Lancing was a public school.

Several of the hut members contributed thoughts to the meeting. Aircraftsman First Class Saul – that wasn't his name but he looked a bit Old Testament and spent the evenings cleaning his feet so that's what we called him – said that it's about ******* time the ******* officers ******* did something for the ******* working lads. Joss said it was a valuable comment and he would make a note of it.

Big John then spoke, which was a bit of an event because he could go a week without saying anything at all. Big John was in the transport unit and was enormous. When there was a really cold spell the hydraulic jacks in the transport unit froze solid so John held the lorries up by their bumpers while the wheels were being changed. 'If we set fire to the hut,' John said thoughtfully, 'It'd be lovely and warm.'

'You stupid ****!' said Saul, amiably. 'We'd all be ******* burnt to ******* death, wouldn't we!'

'Oh, yes,' said John. 'Happen we would, aye.'

'I have already given the problem some thought,' said Joss. 'Larceny will be involved if we are to survive this winter so to protect ourselves from disciplinary action our first step must be to corrupt authority – in the shape of Corporal Wood.'

'That ******' said Saul. 'He's a ******, that's what he ******* is.'

Corporal Wood was a little horror with a pencil moustache. He was in charge of our hut and had a boarded-off bit to himself at one end where he too had to sleep on the floor.

The plan we code-named 'The Unspeakable Corp.' began. I was the station photographer and Joss called on the nearest Icelandic farmhouse and persuaded the farmer to swap a whole churn of fresh milk in exchange for portraits, taken by me, of his loved ones and a couple of cows.

Joss got Big John to persuade his sergeant that one of the lorries needed road-testing, so Joss and John swung the churn of milk on to the back and drove it off to the capital, Reykjavik. In a sports shop in Reykjavik Joss swapped the churn for a lilo, one of those air-bed things which laughing girls fall off at the seaside.

That evening, Joss, Saul and John inflated the lilo (or rather John did. Saul said 'Blow that up? I should ******* cocoa') and presented themselves at the corporal's door. 'What's that?' he said suspiciously, seeing the lilo.

'A small gift, Corp.' said Joss pleasantly. 'From your grateful hut. The floor is so freezing and hard that we thought you would appreciate the considerable comfort of an air bed.' The horrible corporal's little piggy eyes glistened. 'Wassa snag?' he asked.

71

'It's not exactly a gift,' said Joss, softly and pointedly. 'More a loan, really. We shall, of course, try to make our own sleeping arrangements more acceptable. With whatever materials we find to hand . . .'

The dreadful corporal understood perfectly. 'Don't let me see you,' he muttered. 'That's all. If you're nicking Air Force property I don't know anything abart it. Understand?' And he grabbed the lilo and slammed the door.

Joss gave us all our detailed instructions. We had a little bit of practise and that night we swung into action with a demonstration of the degree of unity and precision which the RAF could rise to when faced with adversity which would have struck fear into Hitler's heart.

First of all Big John picked up George, nickname Grease, by his elbows and threw him over the twelve foot high link fence which guarded the transport unit's stores. George was not called Grease because he was slippery but because he used pints of Brylcreem on his hair and was forever combing his great shiny mop and then running the comb between two fingers and squeegeeing off a great blob of grey hair-cream. This he flicked off and had to be dodged, especially at squadron dances. But Grease was highly gifted in another area of human activity – he was one of nature's burglars. He could get in and out of anywhere given a bus ticket and a bit of wire. Having been thrown over the fence he took out his bus ticket and bit of wire and let himself into the transport unit stores and brought out twenty empty square petrol tins which he threw over the wire to us. These were to be the supports for our five beds. He then climbed back over the wire like a monkey and our campaign moved to its next stage, liberating five doors to make the beds themselves.

Joss had worked out a plan of obtaining the doors based upon a well-known principle which he called *L'audace, l'audace, toujours l'audace*' to which Saul replied 'What the **** is that supposed to ******* mean?' and Joss explained that if you act with sufficient affrontery you can get away with anything. So John and Grease turned up at the Squadron Orderly Office in the morning armed with screwdrivers and Joss joined them with a foot rule and a clipboard. Joss measured door-frames busily and jotted down meaningless figures on his clipboard. They unscrewed all the doors of the Squadron's main offices, including those of the adjutant and the

CO, who were working at their desks, without anybody saying anything and bore off the doors to our hut.

Each of us now had a door to lie on, supported well away from the draughty floor. We made mattresses from our dirty clothes and greatcoats and should have slept well.

Except that we were still too cold without fuel for the stove. The solution to this was perhaps Joss's finest hour.

His last card to play was little Ern. Ern was a fairly boring member of the hut because his only interest in life, and that not so much an interest as a fanatical obsession, was doing card tricks. Along, alas, with many professional conjurors he could not stop doing card tricks. In the back of lorries, in the communal loos, at meals in the cookhouse, he would fan out the dirty pack he was never without and then would start: 'choose a card – any card – don't tell me what it is . . .'

But he was good. And the twenty-four hour guard of soldiers mounted over the unfinished huts being built by the Pioneers was grateful for such a diversion from their boredom. So every evening Ern took his cards along to the guard's campfire. And round the back of the unfinished huts Joss and Saul and Grease and Big John and I crept. 'Softly, softly does it,' was Joss's order, so we just quietly wrenched up two floorboards from each hut and chopped them up for firewood. The Pioneers replaced them next day and laid twenty more. We wrenched up just two of these the next night, and so on. The Pioneers never realised.

And so our hut slept on beds draught-free and snug, with a wood fire blazing in the stove all night. Until one day orders came through for the squadron to return to England, where it was dispersed.

It was a long time ago but I will never forget the names of my comrades in that once cold then snugly warm hut in Iceland. I won't forget because I am not allowed to forget. I only have to pass a church during Evensong or watch 'Highway' on the telly and what do I hear but a choir actually singing a roll-call of my friends:

'Ern,
Wood,
Grease,
John,
Saul –
Joss . . .'

'I'm Putting All My Eggs In One Basket'

Popular Song

ONE of the reasons why my purchases at the local vintner rarely go beyond an occasional bottle of Château Under-Three-Quid is my firm belief that more nonsense is written and talked about wine than anything outside of sex. (Assuming, of course, there is anything outside of sex.) I mention that to help you understand exactly how foolish it was for me to make even an attempt at connoisseurship that evening in the Wine Bar.

Have you tried that new Wine Bar on the Parade? Very upmarket, the kind of place that prides itself on being more Mayfair than the West End – you know, the menus all have tassels on the cover, the muzak is the Swingle Singers and the dish of the day is French and made from things you normally only see in autopsy reports. The presiding figure is a tall, white-haired gentleman with the air of an exiled Archduke, and the night we went there he hardly gave us time to sit down before he was at the table with a wine list big enough to project home movies on.

I would have liked an opportunity to study it – or, at least, the right hand column – but it was no sooner in my hand than he'd snatched it back, with the suggestion that perhaps sir would like to leave the selection of the wine to him. He then bowed and departed, returning something less than thirty seconds later with a dusty bottle. After passing it rapidly to and fro in front of my eyes – as though about to perform a trick whereby the label would suddenly change colour – he produced one of those high-tech corkscrews, extracted the cork and handed it to me. Then he stood back, with the cast-down eyes of a modest man about to be extravagantly praised.

I was obviously being invited to offer my opinion of his wine –

74

but was he really expecting me to evaluate it on the basis of just the cork? Admittedly, I have friends who can tell from one sniff of a wine's bouquet whether the peasant who trod the grapes was left-footed or right-footed, but my own knowledge of the various skills wine-samplers have at their disposal is, as I've indicated, less than hazy. Then, suddenly, one of them came to mind. Or, at least, partly to mind – because all I could recall was that it involved something to do with 'swirling it round the inside of your mouth, then spitting it out'. So that's what I did. With the cork.

Have you ever been in a large room when everyone present goes quiet at the same time? That's one of my clearest memories of what happened at that moment. Another is that while I was swirling the cork round inside my mouth, the taste wasn't really at all bad. (Relatively, that is. I mean, compared to the dish of the day.) But the most unforgettable part of the whole episode was the actual moment of spitting it out. The reason being, and there's probably not all that many people who get an opportunity to discover this, a cork can't half *go* . . . You ask that tall white-haired gentleman who was standing there open-mouthed.

Now, I'm not claiming that the episode was something to be proud of. The only reason I'm recounting it is to make the point that when you're a writer all experiences can be grist to your mill. Even when something as embarrasing as that cork thing happens, you can make use of it, transmute it, get a short story out of it, or a novel, or a play, or a three-act verse drama. Or, if you happen to be the kind of writer I am, a short knockabout sketch for the Annual Satirical Revue shortly to be performed by the Golders Green and District Amateur Operatic Society.

Who turned it down! Honestly now, can you believe that? I sent it to them on a Thursday and the following Monday – a day that will live in infamy – I received this letter from their Artistic Director. 'Dear Mr Norman, Thank you for sending us the skit set in a Wine Bar. I regret, however, that we cannot make use of it as I would not wish any of our members to portray a person so oafishly crude and ignorant as to spit a cork at a Wine Waiter. Yours sincerely, Ms Trudy Throng.'

I won't deny that the rejection hit me hard, especially as it was partly my own fault. I should have remembered the Trudy Throng factor, because I knew Ms Trudy Throng when she was Mrs Trudy Throng. That was back in the days when she was married to Al

Throng, a nice chap she dumped the moment the opportunity to take over the Operatic Society came along and he refused to give up his Kenny Ball records. Mind you, that wasn't the offence she cited in the Divorce Court. No, her official case against Al was based on what her lawyer described as his 'distressing and demeaning personal habits': using her electric toothbrush to scratch his back, drinking mayonnaise through a straw, publicly shaming her at the Royal Ballet by shouting, 'That's the way to fill them tights, Mikhail!'; that kind of thing.

While agreeing that such lapses would rate high on anyone's crassness scale, I happened to know Al had engineered all of them deliberately, having long nursed an urge to, as we say in the world of Television, 'switch to another channel'. In this he had been so successful, he and his new partner had not only remained Golders Green residents, they had even become members of the Operatic Society themselves.

So it required only a minimum of co-operation from Al, plus a couple of muttered words in some other right places, to get the stain of rejection wiped from my little sketch's record. For, sure enough, before the end of that week, I received another communication from La Throng, this time a telegram. It was to inform me that she had now decided to accept my work, having been reminded that there was someone at hand who would have no difficulty at all acting 'oafishly crude and ignorant'. Her ex-husband.

The news came as such a relief, I think I can still remember the text of that telegram word for word. Let's see . . .

'I'm putting Al, my "ex", in Wine Bar skit.'

The Light That Failed

Rudyard Kipling
Title of novel

RUDYARD KIPLING knew my great-uncle.
When Kipling made a trip to England he always visited my great-uncle, bringing him some small gift from India, like a see-through dhoti in the colours of the Royal Lancashire Fuseliers or a poppadum. My great-uncle's name was Jedediah but Kipling, with his delightful (and much underrated) sense of humour, always called him Robinson. My great-uncle often referred to Kipling as Ruddy, but not, of course, when Kipling was within earshot, or in England. My great-aunt's name was Fay (Kipling always addressed her as Mrs Robinson). Before she married she was a Butcher.

The reason I mention that Ruddy Kipling knew my great-uncle is that, quite unwittingly, the caption of a photograph belonging to my great-uncle suggested a book-title to Kipling which was so inspiring that he immediately caught a cab to Delhi (via Tilbury docks) and wrote the book, which told the story of a painter who gradually lost both his gift for painting and his eyesight. The phrase which inspired him to write the novel was, of course – *The Light That Failed.*

'But who, or what, was on the photograph? Why did the caption only "suggest" the book title? Come along, you old rogue, out with it! What a story you have to tell!' I hear the reader exclaim with boyish enthusiasm. 'The yarn will be a most welcome addition to the harmless stock of public pleasure as well as a true antidote to so-called television!' I hear you exclaim warmly, slightly overdoing it.

Well, this is what great-uncle Jedediah told Rudyard Kipling that evening, while great-aunt Fay stood next to the walnut what-not tenderly clasping a framed photograph of eight clergymen rowing a racing skiff.

77

The series of events occured on my great-uncle and great-aunt's wedding-day. The marriage was to be solemnised in Southwark Cathedral.

It was an Autumn morning; warm with a light mist. My great-uncle arrived very early at the Cathedral with his best man and sat in the front pew quietly concentrating on making his moustache grow, confident that his bride-to-be was a wholly competent lady in all respects and could be trusted to arrive on time.

About the same moment, my great-aunt-to-be Fay's father, Mr Butcher (who really *was* a butcher), leaving his pleasant cottage in Camberwell, walked his daughter, quite beautiful in her white crinoline wedding-dress, across the main Camberwell Green road to the elegant landau waiting to take them to the Cathedral.

Although no trams were yet running, a tramway system had been laid in South London. It was the earliest design of tramway which had no overhead cables. Instead, a metal rail was sunk into the road between the tramlines and this rail was split in two with an inch or so gap between its halves. Into this gap the tram dangled a metal rod which picked up its electricity.

Fay trod on this split rail and the high heel of her left shoe went down into the slot and would not come out again.

She could have left her shoe behind but she simply could not face the prospect of hopping down the aisle of Southwark Cathedral or bobbing up and down on one shoe.

Fay and her father heaved frantically but the shoe would not come out. Examining the shoe more closely, she saw that because the heel was much narrower in its middle, it moved sideways in the slot quite easily. She decided to walk as quickly as she could manage all the way to the tram depot, sliding her shoe along in the slot, and slip it out of the rail when she came to the end of the line.

She knew there was a depot just built at Southwark, quite near the Cathedral, so she sent her father on ahead in the landau and began to make her way as quickly as she could along the tramway, keeping her left leg rigid to let the heel slide better in the rail. Few of the people out shopping in the streets took any notice of her; they took it for granted that she was just another runaway bride with a wooden leg who had had second thoughts at the altar.

It was when she was barely two miles or so away from Southwark and wedlock, and going well, that she met the points. There was a confluence of tramlines at Stockwell Junction and points were set in the tracks. And the points were arranged to send her tram straight up Stockwell High Street. And so straight up Stockwell High Street, willy-nilly, sped great-aunt-to-be Fay.

The weather was worsening. The autumnal mist had turned into quite a thick fog. Fay, as she was on tramlines, so to speak, and in no danger of wandering into a lampost, was soon joined by elderly fog-bound shoppers who held on to the train of her wedding-dress and on to each other's waists eventually forming a crocodile which, according to the *Morning Post* reached an estimated length of a mile and three quarters.

She got her foot clear at the Upper Norwood tram terminus. There was a turntable there and a couple of trainee tram drivers kindly wound the turntable round a bit and slid her off the rail as easily as sliding a curtain-ring off a pole.

Fay was almost totally exhausted by her ordeal and collapsed thankfully into a parked hansom cab which she had glimpsed through the swirling fog. 'Southwark Cathedral, driver,' she called up through the hatch, 'And please hurry! For I am to be married at three pm!'

'Swipe me blimey, miss!' cried the driver (for he was a cockney). 'I cannot go nowhere in such a thick alsation dog, that is to say, fog, strike a light! Not unless I've got a man walking in front of my dressed crab, that is to say, cab, to show me where to go, cor stone the crows!'

Resourceful as ever, plucky Fay did not hesitate. '*I'll* walk in front of your cab!' she cried in ringing tones.

And she did, too. She walked as fast as she could but she could hardly make out the road in front of her, let alone signposts saying 'Southwark'. The hansom crept along behind her, the horse whinnying with fear and clinging to her hair with its teeth.

Suddenly, as quickly as it had descended, the fog lifted. Which was a good thing as they found that they were on the towpath of the Thames at Twickenham and just about to walk into the river.

But how, thought Fay, am I to get to Southwark from here? The Cathedral is on the river to be sure, but the towpath is far too narrow for a cab to drive along.

She paid off the cab, giving the driver a generous tip for being so obliging in such awful weather, and sat down on the grass to consider her problem.

Suddenly she heard watery swishing noises, a piping voice

79

shouting 'In – OUT! In – OUT!' and round the bend at great speed sped a rowing eight, propelled by eight brawny figures clad in black, with a tiny cox shouting at them. And they were proceeding down-river. Where lay Southwark.

Resourceful as ever, Fay leaped to her feet and hailed the rowers. 'Oi!' she shouted. 'TAXI!'

They were lay brothers from the Roman Catholic college at Strawberry Hill, just up-river. Fay explained to them her desperate plight. In a moment they had thrown the cox overboard and Fay was in his seat, holding the reins. The eight beefy lay brethren leant on their oars with a will and the sleek craft almost flew through the water towards Jedediah and married bliss.

After the marriage ceremony, my great-uncle persuaded the official photographer to bear his tripod and camera to the river's edge and take an archival photograph of the gallant rowers who had responded to Fay's call for help and made the marriage possible.

It was the simple caption to this photograph, written boldly in Jedediah's hand, which suggested to Rudyard Kipling the title for his novel. It read:

'The lay eight that Fay hailed.'

'You and the Night and the Music'

Title of popular song

STRANGE, but to this day I can never hear those
words without recalling Beryl and Her Dancing Chickens. In case
some of you find that reference slightly obscure, let me fill in a little
of its background.

Not long after the war, when Frank and I were just starting in
the script writing trade, we used to lunch every day in a little caff
off Lower Regent Street where many of the Variety agents of that
era foregathered. It didn't take long before they not only allowed us
access to their table-talk – which included the sort of show-business
anecdotes that would make Jackie Collins blush – but, more
importantly, we were taken into the confidence of somebody we
became very fond of, an agent called Harry Pink.

To describe Harry as small-time would have been to inflate his
status in that world. Invariably dressed in an electric-blue mohair
suit that suffered from what could be called 'iron deficiency', he
exuded a kind of doleful optimism that never failed to win our
affection. Mind you, the more he told us about the roster of no-
hopers who had entrusted their fortunes to his guidance, the easier
it became to sympathise with that attitude.

Reciting his list of acts was like sounding a knell for the funeral
of Variety. After so many years I can't remember many of their
names – the only one that, for obvious reasons, seems to be
ineradicable was George Berkinshaw ('Soprano Extraordinaire') –
but I do recall that among them was a ventriloquist who couldn't
even *think* without moving his lips, a comedian who told a succession
of 'knock-knock' jokes with the aid of trained woodpecker, somebody called Ahmed Mahmed ('Scotland's Only Xylophone Playing
Snake Charmer'), and a lady contortionist who, one melancholy

Friday Second House at Dewbury Empire, bent backwards to grasp the back of her ankles, found she had 'locked' in that position and had to be rolled off the stage like a hoop.

Although it was always a tale of calamity Harry had for us, none was ever a tale of defeat. A typical instance was an act called The Three Grinling Brothers who had threatened to leave him and go to another agent unless he got them a recording contract. As Harry related it to us – 'I'll exert my best endeavours,' I said to them. 'But it's not going to be easy. Those recording companies aren't handing out contracts so freely these days. And what you have to remember is,' I said, 'You are, after all, acrobats.'

The point is that he *did* exert his best endeavours – because that was his way – and when he failed, he simply shrugged those electric blue shoulders and began phoning around to try and get them a radio series.

But even more characteristic of his refusal to acknowledge defeat were the battles he undertook on behalf of the group of performers alluded to previously, Beryl and Her Dancing Chickens. Does anybody remember that act? Fourteen Buff Orpingtons and eight Wynadottes, all executing a faltering counter-march as Beryl played a rousing chorus of *St Louis Blues* on her piano accordion.

They were a fairly un-household name even in those days but Harry's respect for their artistry was total. 'You've got to go and see the act,' he kept urging us. 'I promise you, it's your kind of thing. Absolute poultry in motion!'

The strange thing is, there was one fleeting moment when we might well have got to see them, thanks to a quite extraordinary cock-up. While that may not be the most felicitous term to use in connection with performing chickens, there is no other way to decribe the process by which Beryl's flock were invited to appear at the Royal Albert Hall in a United Nations Gala Concert.

The invitation took even Harry by surprise. Over the past six months, he had spent every lunch-hour telling us about the low state of the act's fortunes – in all that time, the only firm enquiry he'd had about them had come from Colonel Sanders – but now, out of the blue, this! With justifiable pride, he showed us a copy of the complete line-up for the proposed Gala Concert. It certainly made impressive reading: Tito Gobbi, Dame Myra Hess, the Amadeus String Quartet, The London Symphony Orchestra and Beryl & Her Dancing Chickens.

Of course, by the next day, somebody had twigged the mistake and well before any posters could be printed, Harry was in receipt of an official letter. 'Sincere apologies, administrative error, extremely sorry, inexcusable mistake, deeply regret, not really in keeping, please accept enclosed pair of complimentary tickets,' etc.

Nothing has ever defined old-time show-business for me like Harry's reaction to that letter. He simply refused to acknowledge the possibility that it might have something to do with his artistes. 'Do these people think I can't recognise an alibi when I see one?' he raged, over the following lunchtime's small egg mayonnaise. 'It's not our chickens they consider too low-brow for the venue. It's that tune they dance to – the *St Louis Blues*. What those old buffers running the place won't stand for is having a *jazz* number played at the Albert Hall.'

His blistering letter of protest to *The Stage* appeared in its correspondence columns the following week. Running to over 2000 words, the substance of it was an impassioned reiteration of his lunchtime allegations. The move by certain vested interests to oust his talented livestock was no more than an underhand way of preventing the Albert Hall audience – and thus, by extension, the United Nations itself – from hearing the most popular composition the grand old tunesmith W. C. Handy ever wrote.

It was Harry's finest hour and *The Stage* did him proud by allocating his letter an apt headline. Clear across the top of the page ran the words –

U.N. Denied Handy Music

Polyurethane

A synthetic resin used in varnishes

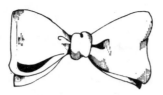

T HERE is something splendidly British about a village pageant. It is so Christian in its aim to bring pleasure to the community, so unselfish in the amount of time and energy freely given by the participants, and so certain to disintegrate into malevolent vendettas which split happy families into warring factions and cause a sharp upward swing in the cottage hospital's intake of found-drunk-and-incapables, nervous collapses and victims of assault and battery perpetrated after rehearsals by loved ones. The effect on a village community of staging a pageant is equal to a vistation of the Black Death.

Black Death – in the shape of 'THORPE DOWN THE AGES. Our Village Through the Centuries, tickets 30p and 45p from the Post Office Stores or, if closed, Mrs Rumbold' – visited my village about twelve years ago.

The guilty men, towards whom the chicken bone should be pointed, were my son Jamie and Vicar, The Revd. Nicholas Menon (known to all as Nick the Vic).

Jamie was going to direct the pageant, which was to take place in the church, using the aisles and the chancel and the apse as the stage in the modern manner. Nick the Vic was to co-write the pageant with Jamie. They were aiming for a working partnership along the lines of Burbage and Shakespeare. Nick the Vic was a gifted writer but his skills ran mainly to writing metaphysical verse of a high quality in the manner of John Donne or fairly fruity, black farce in the style of Evelyn Waugh's *Vile Bodies*, neither of which styles was wholly suited to 'THORPE DOWN THE AGES'.

It was their inexperience as producers of pageants which was the basic snag, but then *all* producers of pageants are inexperienced. Nobody – but nobody – ever produces a village pageant twice.

Now, twelve years later, angers have more or less cooled and I'm able to reveal that it was the last minute appearance of my dear wife, Polly, which saved the evening. Because of Polly, the pageant is now remembered as being a sickening disappointment but not a total disaster.

It all began to go wrong before it had properly started. Nick the Vic announced plans for the Pageant in the pulpit one Sunday, pointing out that it was a project to involve the entire village, not only the Dramatic Society.

'If you want to be in it you *shall* be in it!' cried Nick the Vic (Shakespeare) recklessly. 'I shall write each and every one of you a special part.' Carried away in his boyish enthusiasm Nick had forgotten the Golden Rule of amateur dramatics which states: those who *can* act, won't; those who volunteer are entirely without any kind of talent whatsoever.

The first get-together and casting session was organised to take place in the village hall. Some sixty bright-eyed, pitifully keen and totally ungifted souls turned up. Some of them, even if in an emergency, were unable to speak louder than a whisper and were inaudible six feet away. Others could project their voices in a thrilling wall of sound which was audible in the Red Lion half a mile a way but it was not possible to distinguish one word from another. A number were afflicted with speech impediments. Three of the volunteers were newcomers to the village and their turbans presented a casting problem. One lady spoke only in French.

Jamie (Burbage) got to work organising them. He first divided them into two groups, a few to each century, with instructions to devote all their spare time during the coming weeks to making their costumes. One group was to be assorted gentry and the other to be humble villagers.

All those appointed to be gentry entered into the spirit of the thing and pranced about the hall going: 'Fie, milady, 'pshaw!', and 'Bring wine, varlet!'. Those cast as humble villagers went very quiet, left the hall shortly afterwards and subsequently sent in letters of resignation.

Nick the Vic and Jamie spread charm and affability and lies and got most of the humble villagers back but it was clear that the swineherds and maidservants were going to be up-market or nothing. The peasant costumes they knocked up, which historically were sacking and odd rags, were amazing. The lady playing old Mrs Toft, the eighteenth century crone in Guildford who pretended she had given birth to a litter of rabbits, prinked on stage looking like Barbara Cartland, bejewelled, in rosy-beige.

Jamie and Nick, having got the cast sorted out and – however unsuitably – clad, then turned to compiling the script. They borrowed *The History of Chertsey and Thorpe* from the Chertsey Museum and bore it off home with a view to selecting the very best events, the most dramatic items, to make for a really gripping pageant.

This is when the second blow fell. The history of Thorpe took up a page and a half of the book. Nothing had happened in Thorpe. Not just nothing – *absolutely* nothing had *ever* happened, either in, about, or near Thorpe. It had just squatted, a smallish village, in the shadow of the great medieval abbey of Chertsey with nothing happening in it for century after century.

Eventually Burbage and Shakespeare saved the day. On the night of the pageant they put me into clergyman's clothes and I stood in the pulpit (ill with fatigue having been filming all day) reading out the non-story of Thorpe while the villagers illustrated the passing years with mimes of various activities. The script was a masterpiece of speciousness and audience manipulation.

Highlights, I recall, included:

Me (*half-asleep, reading from script*): '1543, the year of the Great Freeze. The Thames froze over. So would have done the duckpond in Coldharbour Lane, where Thorpe villagers would have enjoyed themselves in traditional village winter sports:'

ENTER prosperous-looking serfs who pretend to skate and fall over amusingly.

Me: 'In 1603 All England celebrated the crowning of its new monarch, James 1. And the villagers of Thorpe, poor though they were, would not have been left out of the patriotic revelry:'

ENTER richly-dressed poor villagers who sit in a circle while Charlene Legg (aged 9, daughter of Councillor Legg,

86

Indpenedent Rate-Payers) obliges with her tap dance to the music of 'West Side Story'.

Then real disaster struck. Our big finish was King John signing the Magna Carta (Runnymede is only a few miles away). King John (Mrs Dean), surrounded by Knights and Earls, will not sign. Suddenly a vast, hairy Thane from the Scottish delegation springs forward with his claymore upraised. King John screams in fear and signs. The whole cast cheers, we fade up the music and the whole cast links arms and sings 'You'll Never Walk Alone', swaying.
Curtain.

The trouble was that our Thane, the enormous Pete, had developed stage fright and during the first half had popped over to the Red Lion for a stiffener. By half way through the second half he was so stiff that they had to take him home in a hired car.

I was the first to notice he was missing from the final scene. I slipped out of the pulpit and went backstage. There was his costume lying in a heap but no him. And there was my wife Polly, prompting through a gap in the curtain.

In a flash I had flung the great Scottish cloak over Polly's frail shoulders – it drooped along the ground like Dopey's – put the mighty claymore in her hand and pushed her towards the stage entrance.

'You're our big, glossy finish!' I said. 'On you go!'

'How do you mean? Who am I supposed to *be*, dressed in all this stuff?'

I explained. Quietly, simply:

'Polly – you're a Thane'.

Things that go bump in the night

From an old Scottish prayer

A LARGE body of literature has grown up around the legendary figure of King Arthur, some of it dating back as far as the sixth century. But in none of the accounts, not even the important *Mabinogion*, or William of Malmesbury's *Gesta Regum Anglorum*, will you find any mention of one of my ancestors, a commoner or villein named Mostyn Norden, who occupied the position of official tailor to King Arthur's court.

The reason I find that omission so singularly galling is that if ever there was a person who deserved to be enshrined in song and story, it was Great-uncle Mostyn. Not only was he Camelot's most successful Men's Outfitter, with branches in Avalon, Glastonbury and throughout Cornwall, but he made a unique contribution to all the activities for which the Knights of the Round Table have since become so renowned, such as rescuing virgins from fire-breathing dragons. (I hasten to reassure those of a nervous disposition that nowadays such creatures are, of course, quite extinct. So, for that matter, are dragons.)

It was Uncle Mostyn who advised Arthur that only one form of Men's Suiting would stand up to the demands made by those exacting forms of rescue work. Whether for business or leisure wear, the answer had to be armour. And, before long, every member of the Round Table who liked his suit of armour to be both smart and comfortable knew that nobody in the entire Dark Ages could make him one like my Uncle Mostyn.

There was a craftsmanship in the man, a pride in his trade, that evinced itself the moment you entered the small forge that served as his cutting room. 'Take a look at this,' he would say, bringing out a length of material for your inspection. 'Lovely bit of metal, that.

Wear like iron. Is it a special occasion you're needing the suit for, sir, may I ask? Ah, a sword joust . . . Very nice – but, in that case, I better not make the sleeves so short this time. Don't want you getting a hand chopped off just because you like a bit of cuff showing.'

At the first fitting, for which he would visit you at your own castle, there would be the same skilled eye for detail. 'Put on a bit of weight, I notice,' he'd say, expertly chalking a rivet here, a bolt there. 'Probably be wise to change your shield-size to the next one up. Oh, be no trouble at all, sir, I started in this business supplying protective clothing for the fuller figure. We called it "The Pudgy Armour Game". Now, while we're at it – what about something nice for the wife? I've had a delivery of some lovely white samite. Mystic! Wonderful!'

But despite that intimate involvement with the very heart of the Arthurian mysteries, will you find one mention of Great-uncle Mostyn in the work of Tennyson or Malory? Let me save you the trouble of searching. They do not accord him as much as a footnote. Not even an asterisk.

Yet this was the man whose influence can be discerned in every aspect of that mythic era. In the legend of Sir Gawain and the Green Knight, for instance, who do you think persuaded Gawain's opponent to wear that particular colour? 'Would I lie to you?' Great-uncle Mostyn said to him. 'Black is out this year. You wear black, you'll look more like a squire than a knight. Whereas green . . . Green'll do wonders for your cuirass.'

For that was something else my distinguished forebear introduced to the Court: 'armourial accoutrements'. With every bespoke suit of armour a knight ordered, he could also purchase such useful accessories as a loin-guard, or a hauberk, or an early form of windscreen-wiper for his visor; even a small patch to stick on a steed's haunches saying, 'We've been to see Morgan Le Fay'.

But those did not represent Great-uncle Mostyn's most valued contribution to life at the court of the hero-king. I have left that till last only because it entails drawing your attention to the way a person's life *changes* when he is obliged to spend the major portion of each day inside a suit made of overlapping metal plates. While there are certain activities a man in those circumstances must resign himself to giving up more or less completely – skin-diving is the one that comes most immediately to mind – I wonder if you can guess which of them places him at the biggest disadvantage?

There was no doubt about which one the Camelot *wives* considered most tiresome. In a survey carried out in the year 410 AD, they unanimously confirmed it was the clanking and clattering in the middle of the night when their husbands were obliged to get out of bed and go to the thing in full armour. Bearing in mind that, in those days, every castle room had a stone floor, particularly the smallest one, those of you with paving stones on your patio can gain some idea what that nocturnal clangour must have sounded like by going out there with an armful of metal saucepans and tin trays, then dropping them to the ground in small batches. Better still, try doing it at three or four in the morning. Besides duplicating almost exactly what those mediaeval households had to put up with, it could also help you get to know your neighbours.

I would contend that in ridding his world of that particular affliction, Great-uncle Mostyn placed himself every bit as much in the mainstream of Arthurian legend as Guinevere or Uther Pendragon. How did he accomplish it? By the invention of what became known as his 'Quick Ejection' model, a suit of armour so designed that with one twist of a small attachment, any parfit, gentil knight could step out the back of it in a trice – leaving the suit standing perfectly upright!

Surely that in itself is enough to have earned him at least a chapter in *The Once And Future King*. After all, he did finally put an end to what was, by common consent of every Arthurian scholar, the most disagreeable aspect of the Camelot era –

Knights that go bump in the thing.

Around The World In Eighty Days

Novel by Jules Verne
Film version of the novel

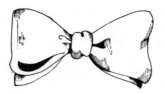

I AM not an astonishing sort of person. Some people are, and I envy them. They are pointed out at parties and are the subject of colourful whisperings: 'Do you remember years ago reading about a titled policeman who swam the Irish Channel naked for a bet and later married a beautiful Javanese pearl-diver – well, that's the titled ex-policeman in the corner, the elderly lady filling her handbag with the cheese straws. He had the operation in Morocco.'

There is absolutely nothing riveting like that to be whispered about me at a party. The most dramatic that could be said would be along the lines of 'Look at that tall man with hiccoughs – I think he's sat in something.'

This total absence of glamorous incident in my life never worried me because nobody knew or cared enough about my past to want to know details of it – to me a CV was something that the tiny little French Citröen car had only *deux* of. Then one day, in California, USA, the blow fell.

I was on an author tour promoting a book and I was in the office of a researcher attached to a television programme in which, for a consideration of a million dollars a week, a man in a sharp suit chatted semi-affably to guests and made some little jokes. She was weighing me up as a potential guest.

This programme did not seem to me to be a good place to try to sell books as any viewer literate enough to read the programme's title would switch it off, but my publisher said it was a very important contactual outlet.

'Tell me everything about yourself,' said the researcher, a lady with much, much too much bright orange hair and a voice like football studs on plate glass. 'Y'know, all those cute damn things you done like at school and y'know. Those crazy antics you British get up to, right? Total recall, Mister, is the name of this game so go, go, go.'

I could not think of anything at all. Like a drowning man, which professionally I was, my life passed before my eyes on Fast Forward. But it was, as far as crazy antics were concerned, incidentless.

'There was,' I said eventually, 'a dramatic moment during a school Sports Day. I had developed a blister on my heel and I took my running shoe off to air the blister and I left my running-shoe on a deck-chair, *spikes-uppermost!*'

'And what happened?' cried Tangerine, ball-point poised.

'Well, nothing *happened*.' I explained. 'I just thought it was an interesting thing to have done. After cooling my blister I put the shoe back on and had a lemonade.'

Tangerine looked at me for quite a long time without blinking. She clicked the ball-point pen with her thumb and the bit with the ball withdrew from sight. I felt the interview was not going well.

'Look, mister,' she said. 'Have you got *anything* to talk about which will make fifty million American viewers watch you rather than switch over to a nude movie on cable-TV, ferchrissake?'

Spurred by the urgency of matters, inspiration at last struck.

'I don't drink tea!' I gasped.

'Hot dickerty-dee!' said the lady, 'Hold the front page!'

'But why don't I drink tea? The answer to that intriguing question, madam, is the story of the one exciting thing that has happened to me in my whole life. And the whole incredible, colourful, bizarre adventure is substantiated in a press-cutting from the *Canterbury and Weald of Kent Messenger* which I have preserved to this day pressed in lavender in my hanky drawer.'

'This is not happening to me,' the lady said.

I was aged twelve at the time of the adventure. We lived in Broadstairs, Kent, and I was deeply in love with a girl named Gentian Leatherbarrow (her parents kept the stationery shop next to the chemists in York Street).

Gentian was not a great conversationalist. She had a working vocabulary of about fifteen stock phrases which, when you took away 'Does this train stop at Margate?' and 'Pass the marmalade' did not leave her much in the way of general conversation. She had kindly reserved two phrases to be used exclusively during our precious moments together. They were of a sceptical nature and ran 'Oh, yeah?' and 'That'll be the day'.

I was desperate to pierce her scepticism. 'I'll prove myself to you,' I said one evening, breaking the silence as we leant against the fish shop window. 'I will show you that I am incredibly brave to the point of being foolhardy.'

'Oh, yeah,' she said.

'You're going to be proud of me.'

'That'll be the day,' she said.

I hitched up my trousers (I had no hips at all then).

A week later my form went on a nature ramble to the Weald of Kent where there was always a lot of nature going on. Near where the bus dropped us on the outskirts of Penshurst I noticed a huge and peculiar wooden structure in a field, like an enormous round water-tank. Then I saw a notice which said that the field was the winter quarters of a travelling fair. The wooden structure was a Wall of Death, now weather-beaten and battered with its planks loosened by years of motor-bikes roaring round its inside.

At that moment I knew what a man had to do.

The following evening I broke the silence as Gentian and I leaned against the cake shop wall.

'If you will kindly catch the three o'clock bus to Penshurst next Wednesday afternoon, Gentian,' I said, 'You will see in a field near the bus stop a curious circular wooden wall.'

'Oh, yeah,' she said.

I hitched my trousers up.

'What is more,' I said, 'If you watch you will see I, your lover – defying gravity and at the risk of his personal life – Riding the Wall of Death!'

'That'll be the day,' she said.

I planned it all carefully. I did not own a bicycle so I had to borrow one. Everybody was using theirs on a free Wednesday afternoon so I had to settle for hiring a tiny fairy cycle at a large fee from the small but venal girl next door. I found it difficult to ride being so tall but I could get along reasonably well as long as I did not slow down.

I took the early bus to Penshurst. The Wall looked very large and daunting close-up. There was a door in the wall for getting in. I made a mental note to close it behind me.

I felt so nervous that I went to a transport cafe along the road and had a mug of tea. It was very strong tea and I felt wobbly after it. The tea was dark and thick. The time for Gentian's bus came and she was not on it so I had another two or three mugs of tea as I waited for the next bus. I began to feel really peculiar – light-headed and elated.

What I did not know then was that I am allergic to the tannin in tea. I now know that it overstimulates me to a dangerous degree.

I went into a pink haze and I could hear my blood bubbling. I wanted to thresh about, to run up a mountain, to GO!

I ran out of the cafe, grabbed my niece's fairy cycle and ran with it into the Wall of Death, slamming the door behind me. I pumped at the pedals with my vast feet and I and the bike shot round the Wall and up it, my legs going like pistons. And round and round and up and down I raced.

On my fifth circuit Gentian arrived. I was approaching the door at an incredible speed when she opened it from the outside. Out into the Great Weald of Kent I on the fairy cycle shot like a bullet.

Police cars were called in to give chase. Army helicopters hovered. I continued to pedal furiously on a compulsive tour of villages whose names were only a blur: St Leonards, Ashdown, Leith Hill . . .

Nowadays I sometimes doubt whether my one adventure ever really happened. But on those occasions I only have to open my hanky drawer, brush aside the dried lavender and there is my evidence. Staring up at me is the *Messenger*'s headline:

AROUND THE WEALD IN A TEA DAZE

'Hail to thee, blithe spirit, bird thou never wert'

Shelley's 'To A Skylark'

GATHER round, me hearties, and I'll spin you a tale of long-ago, or perhaps even a bit before that. I'm talking about the time I served as cabin boy aboard the good ship *Bounty*, bound for the Coconut Isles.

A proud, beautiful four-master she were when first she was commissioned, with spanking white topsails and a great curved figurehead of an undressed lady jutting out in front, Bristol-fashion. But at the time of which I'm relating, she'd turned into a right hell-ship. Her mains'ls were all tattered, the futtocks were worm-eaten, the fo'c's'le had lost two of its apostrophes and even the life-belts had big holes in the middle.

But none of us dared complain, not when the master of the ship were Captain Bligh. Oh, a right slave-driver he were, a giant of a man with a voice that could warp a nine-inch teak plank, and the cruellest notions of seafaring in the British Navy. Besides the usual keel-haulings and mast-lashings, he used to inflict prow-draggings, hatch-bashings, bilge-crawlings and bulwark-tuggings, to say nothing of the order he once pinned up to throw the bos'n overboard when what he'd meant to write was 'basin'.

All this went alongside the food he gave us to live on. A disgrace to human digestion that was, what with dumplings that tasted like boiled door-knobs, rissoles we sometimes used to scour the deck with, and meatballs so heavy, we used to throw 'em to the sea-gulls, then count how many sank. And all the while, he sat below in his cabin, dining off the finest napery Cookie could fry up, and occupying his time making little model shipwrecks in bottles.

Where it all boiled up to a head was when we got to South of the Azores and found ourselves becalmed; floating motionless in what the Admiralty manuals call a 'no-wind' situation.

'Closehaul your ratlines!' screams Bligh. Then, when that doesn't whistle up as much as a breath of wind, 'Put the rudder midships and double reef your topmast studding-sail boom!'

But nothing worked. He even tried the old nautical trick of tossing overboard a selection of French cheeses – some say it encourages the offshore bries – but when even that failed, he became so impatient he set in hand his own method of getting the ship moving forward. He sent the whole ship's company topside, made us line up on the poop-deck, then ordered all of us to *blow* on the sails.

Well, as you can imagine, after three solid days and nights of doing this, some of the crew were so exhausted, they hardly had the breath left to cool their cocoa. And that were when Fletcher Christian started talking mutiny.

A strange one he were, that Fletcher Christian, a more educated man nor the rest of us, as you could tell by the habit he had of blowing his nose in a handkerchief. 'Will you come aft with me, lad?' he said on the fourth morning we were becalmed, soon after Bligh had given the chaplain 30 strokes of the lash on the accusation he'd been sucking instead of blowing.

'Come where?' I asks, for by then I were that dropping with fatigue, I hardly knew my aft from my bowsprit.

'To the parrot's cage,' answers Christian – and I caught on immediately what way his thoughts were tending.

If there was one thing Fletcher Christian hated Bligh for more than anything else, it was the way he treated his parrot. There was this parrot Bligh kept in his cabin, to give him something to swear at while he was bottling his shipwrecks. Wretched, depressed creature it looked, and you could tell how scared of Bligh it was by the way it would huddle up in a corner of its cage and use the little mirror to try and send SOS messages.

But even worse than that, to Fletcher's educated way of thinking, was that Bligh was so pig-ignorant he didn't even realise it was a parrot. He thought it were one of them seabirds they call an albatross. What's more, clodhead that he was, he lived under the impression that was spelled 'Albert Ross'. So he christened the bird 'Albert', a name which by now he'd shortened to 'Bert'.

Well, I can't tell you how that got up Fletcher Christian's nose. Him being so well-read, you see, he recognised immediately that the parrot was female. And to have Bligh continually calling a female 'Bert' – well, to him, it was like insulting Womanhood;

which your educated classes, of course, they deny themselves that pleasure.

So it was that parrot which stiffened Fletcher Christian's resolve. He assembled the rest of the lower-deck members by the wheelhouse – rallying them with the promise, 'I'll get Bligh with a little help from my friends' – then off we all swarmed to the ship's galley where we armed ourselves with belaying pins and marlin spikes, implements the cook had been using to tenderise the meat. We then made for the quarterdeck and before you could say 'Bobby Shaftoe!', we had old Bligh off the ship and drifting astern of us in the bumboat.

His voice were purple with anger as he shook his fist at us and shouted, 'Cast me adrift in an open boat, would you! Almost two thousands yards from the nearest land! And without even my Albert Ross for company!'

'Once and for all,' Fletcher shouts back, 'She is *not* and never has been an albatross!' And turning to the bird, he uttered some words I shall never forget if I live to be mayor of Pitcairn.

Tenderly stroking its beak, he said –

'Hail to thee, Bligh's parrot. 'Bert' thou never wert.'

The Way To The Stars

Title of film

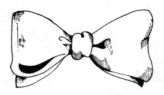

A CHAP I know – perhaps you know him too? – goes by the name of Rollo? – feeble-looking publisher? – face goes spotty under strip lighting? – lives in Bagshot? – two children and a wife called Fonzy who is emotionally involved with dolphins, lead-free petrol and Gordon's gin? Ring a bell?

No? Well. Anyway, Rollo, who publishes magazines with titles like *Which Tool?* and *Second-hand Pram Buyer's Price Guide*, has become so rich from these achingly dull publications that he wants to start a more interesting magazine. So he invited my lady wife and me to his lovely home in Bagshot for dinner to pick our brains. Fonzy is keen on cooking and Rollo wondered whether there might be a market for a different kind of *Good Food Guide* such as *The Guide to Really Simple Food*.

The dinner was fried yoghurt with a curry and Pernod sauce followed by swan *en croute* with yams and caviare butter and a Dom Perignon champagne sorbet. The coffee beans were flown in (weekly) from La Paz, Bolivia.

It was a horrible evening.

Looking back on it, as one does on the drive home when the affronts are still warm, we listed the pleasure-spoiling aspects of our dinner out.

The lovely home in Bagshot was on the main road next to a bus stop so we had to park in a field next door and pick our way back to the house through thick mud. The dining room had a vast open fireplace upon which Rollo had proudly flung, and set fire to, half an elm tree. It was a warm April evening and by the time the sorbet arrived the room temperature was in the region of one hundred and four degrees Fahrenheit. Rollo and Fonzy's children had a scratch meal upstairs but were allowed to watch videos of their choice, which were rock and roll bands at full volume. Down below we could *just* keep the conversation going by choosing simple words and screeching.

And Rollo and Fonzy turned out to be deadly boring. We knew Rollo was but we had hopes that the gin might transform Fonzy and make her strip off and dance on the table or fall down – do *something* to brighten up the evening – but the gin had the opposite effect and she sank into a resentful silence.

Then, in the car, a great truth dawned upon us. Food – however superb – is just *one* factor in the enjoyment of an evening out and the delights of fine food can be cancelled by the other factors not coming up to scratch, e.g., if parking the car is tiresome and inconvenient, if the restaurant gets unpleasantly hot as the evening progresses, if the tables are too close together and the noise level becomes intrusive. And, perhaps worst of all, if nothing odd or funny happens and the evening turns out to be, apart from the food, deadly dull.

There are many books available guiding the punter towards eating-places which serve excellent food, ethnic food, cheap food, even simple good food, but what the world does not have is a publication called something like *The Good Evening-Out Guide* which would recommend restaurants in which the food may be only barely adequate but, much more importantly, parking is easy and the restaurant remains throughout the evening delightfully cool, quiet, and fun.

I was about to ring up Rollo and suggest that this is the book he should publish but my wife grabbed the phone from me in time. If Rollo published it we would have to have dinner with them again.

So my idea is open to any progressively-minded publisher.

Moreover, my wife and I will give the lucky publisher his first recommendation. It is a restaurant which we found by accident in France forty years ago.

The restaurant might well have fallen down twenty years ago but if not, here are the full details:

THE GOOD EVENING-OUT GUIDE
COUNTRY: *France*
VENUE: *Hôtel de la* Something-or-other.
ADDRESS: *Rue du* (forgotten)

Thorigny-sur-Oreuse (I think that was the name
of the village but it might have begun with a
V. Almost impossible to find but if it's any
help it was about an inch below Paris on our
road map).

It was July, 1949, and my bride and I were on our way back from a month's honeymoon in the south of France. This was achieved on the travel allowance then of £45 per person and it is the measure of how the world has changed that the problem then was not how we could last a month in Cannes on £90 (a studio room, food a slice of *veau* and a pocketful of *salade macedoine*) but how on earth we could possibly raise the £90.

We drove in my clapped-out, drop-head Frazer-Nash BMW with a wheel-bearing gone on the rear off-side, which meant motoring a couple of thousand miles with the rear wheel making a noise like a coffee-grinder.

Homeward-bound, golden-brown as a brace of salted peanuts but tired out after driving all day and deafened by the noise of the bearing, we realised as we were approaching Paris that we had just enough money and time left before catching the ferry to have a real meal in a real but very cheap restaurant. So we stopped in this village and saw the Hôtel de la something or other. The menu in the window, in mauve ink, said SOUPE DU JOUR, GIGOT, FROM-AGE. 12F.

This was about our speed. Inside was a bar, and the restaurant was upstairs. When we saw the stairs a little tingle told us that this might be a memorable evening. On many old French staircases the treads are warped and point downwards but this staircase was so ancient and bent that we had to clutch the banister climbing up it. It was like ascending a slippery slope.

Above was the dining-room, two tables, one occupied by a massive, silent couple with a small, fat dog lying under the table, breaking wind. In the corner of the dining-room was a very, very old man, perhaps a hundred years old, bent over and apparently writhing in agony, like a rugger player who has suddenly received the ball in a painful place. He was making little dncing steps and slowly revolving. We watched in awe for quite a few minutes wondering whether we should offer help when there was a 'pop' and the figure straightened up. We saw a wine bottle between his knees and a corkscrew, with cork, in his right hand. He poured wine tremblingly for the massive couple, missing the glasses frequently and watering the paper table cloth red.

Our evening out had started well and it got better.

The soup arrived cold but that did not matter. We heard it coming up the stairs five minutes before it arrived. The ancient waiter had to haul himself up the slippery slope of the stairs by the handrail and his wheezings and muttered Gallic oaths preceded him.

The *Gigot* was a strip of leather baked on to a bone but the cheese was excellent; goatish and deep and lingering, and the bread was French bread, which is the best, at its best.

We descended the stairs, very carefully, with much hanging on to the banisters, for coffee in the bar.

The evening then became even more ejoyable.

We heard the ancient waiter descending. By the thuds and swearing and the clinking we gathered he was carrying down a loaded tray, probably having cleared our table.

There was a loud shout and a rattling of glasses and crockery which we worked out afterwards must have been when the waiter, having got speed up down the sloping stairs, had hit the wall with his shoulder at the turn in the staircase and gone into a spin, accelerating down the last treacherous flight.

A monsieur who was clearly the proprietor was telling a friend at the bar a complicated story about a niece of his, aged 42, who had lost her virtue in the church bell-tower to a Polish student who was on a grape-picking holiday. As the bangs and clinking reached a crescendo the proprietor moved unhurriedly to the front door and, without pausing in his story, opened it. The ancient waiter, bearing his tray, hurtled across the bar-room, spinning, and whizzed out through the door.

The proprietor halted in his narrative a moment to cock his head and listen. There was no screech of brakes, crash of crockery or sounds of a waiter being run over so he resumed telling his story.

Back through the front door crept the ancient waiter, tray intact. He made his way into the kitchen.

So there you are. All the elements of a marvellous evening out. The bread and cheese was tremendously enjoyable. We parked right outside. The room was cool (one of the windows was broken) and peaceful (the other couple never spoke to each other. The only noise came from the dog, and that only intermittently).

And as for entertainment, the vital 'fun' element. That was exemplary and can be summed up for *The Good Evening-Out Guide* in four words:

The waiter! The stairs!

'Show Me The Way To Go Home'

Old drinking song

HOW that phrase brings it back . . .! A chapter in my life called Fifi La Tush.

In those far off days, she earned her living by posing nude for what were then known as 'Art Studies'. As for me, I was an idealistic young would-be dramatist, unsuccessfully hawking my first play round the West End. It was an ambitious work, a blank verse drama about a gang of existential gunmen who hide out in the home of a suburban flower shop owner. It was entitled 'The Petrified Florist' and I was already losing hope of attracting any management's interest in it – couldn't they see it was really a savage allegory on postwar England? – when an envelope dropped through the letter box bearing a floridly designed logo incorporating the initials IMI.

They turned out to stand for 'International Masterpieces Incorporated', a theatrical production company who wanted me to attend at their London Offices as soon as possible, so that I could receive news to my mutual advantage. I was there within the hour, hair glistening with the last of my Brylcreem and a freshly ironed typescript of the play under my arm.

My first disappointment was discovering that their London Offices were the back room of a Surgical Applicances shop in the Charing Cross Road; the second, that their current – and only – production was a touring revue called *Babes and Boobs*. But it was the next item of information that sent my spirits plunging down to basement level. The only reason my presence had been requested was because *Babes and Boobs* needed a cheap writer to come up with some lines of off-stage commentary, to be spoken while its star, the lady known as Fifi La Tush, stood around the stage dressed in differing versions of nothing at all.

Now, this is probably the point where, for the benefit of those of you who were not around in the Fifties, I should explain some of the conventions you had to observe then as regards appearing before an audience without any clothes on. Nowadays, of course, nudity is something that's considered acceptable by practically everybody who performs in public – the only exception I can think of are carol singers – but back then, there was still a certain amount of resistance to it from Watch Committees and the like. So artistes like Fifi were obliged to lend their nude poses a measure of redeeming cultural significance by relating them to various highly regarded paintings.

Which is where the off-stage commentary came in. 'And now,' an unseen male voice would proclaim, 'the beautiful Fifi will render her interpretation of that hand-painted work of art by Van Goya, entitled *Venus Arising From The Foam*.' At which point, the curtain would go up to reveal a large and somewhat grubby papier-mache seashell, inside which Fifi would be crouching, covered from neck to knee in small, opaque soap-bubbles.

'Although the original of this portrayal hangs in the world-famous Prado collection at Uffizzi in Northern Portugal,' the voice would continue, 'art-lovers will be able to purchase photographic postcards of Mademoiselle Fifi's version in the Stalls and Circle bars during the Intermission.' And while the voice of the unseen man behind the curtain would go droning on, the pit orchestra would very softly play *Gems From The Quaker Girl*, Fifi would retain a careful immobility and the eyes of every male member of the audience would hopelessly rove her bubbles for signs of a possible gap.

Soon after I signed the contrtact with IMI, I discovered that the off-stage voice would henceforth be mine. It was something for which, as with so many other misfortunes in my life, I had only myself to blame. Being totally unused to reading the small print of legal documents, I failed to notice that in addition to contracting for the supply of two pages of dignified commentary, I had also bound myself to speak it into the off stage-microphone, as well as 'rendering the artiste such assistance with her props and costumes as may be deemed necessary for the proper performance of her act'.

It was that last requirement which brought the association between Fifi and me to such an unhappy conclusion. Up till then, we had got on well together, mainly thanks to the very real sympathy she displayed towards my dramatic aspirations. (Apparently, one of her grandsons was also of a literary bent.) What our professional partnership foundered on was an unfortunate combination of my habitual absent-mindedness and the vestiges of residual modesty Fifi still nurtured.

I have to admit I found that last characteristic a bit surprising, but her pre-performance preparations made it unmistakeable. Prior to the *Venus Rising From The Foam* number, for instance, she would arrive on stage covered in a brownish coloured raincoat that reached down to her ankles, clamber into her sea-shell and, thus clad, sit quietly until she heard the opening bars of *The Quaker Girl*. Then, in a series of rapid but expert movements, she would slip the raincoat off and throw it towards me, simultaneously catching the aerosol foam-dispenser I tossed her. With this, she would cover herself all over with bubbles and, no more than a second before the curtain rose, lob the foam dispenser back to me.

What finally happened was, I suppose, inevitable. First House one Wednesday, I forgot it. Just plain forgot to bring it on stage with me. The foam dispenser, I mean.

I shall never forget the sound those Old Age Pensioners made when the curtain went up. The collective intake of breaths was so powerful, the heavy house curtains *stirred*. Nor shall I forget the anguished expression on Fifi's face as, for the very first time fully exposed to the public gaze, she muttered to me over and over again the same desperate plea –

'Throw me the spray to blow foam!'

More In Sorrow Than In Anger

William Shakespeare
'Hamlet'

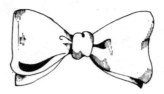

DENIS and I almost became extremely rich some years ago. It was in the early days of a radio show which we were then writing called *Take It From Here*.

It was the immediate post-war period of the early nineteen fifties. Austerity was still with us, which meant that we had clothing coupons entitling us to a quarter ration of six handkerchiefs, three-quarters of a pullover or a sports jacket with one sleeve. And we were constantly being told to 'Export or Perish' by various exporters and perishers.

Then this American producer turned up and wanted to drag us off to the fleshpots of Los Angeles where we could order *two* fried eggs for breakfast at our hotel without being arrested. Plus becoming, almost incidentally, millionaires. Television had just taken off in a big way over there and the making of commercials had become a heavy industry. This American producer had searched England for two chaps whom he needed to advertise suits. It seems that his client was a vast and important company making ready-made, off-the-peg suits which they advertised as coming in all sizes. They claimed to be able to fit *all* customers, however, grotesque their shape.

This American producer chap had called in to the Paris Cinema, Lower Regent Street, one rainy evening thinking that it was a cinema showing saucy French films and discovered that it was not a place of entertainment at all but a BBC studio. What he saw was Denis and me, 'warming-up' the studio audience for a recording of *Take It From Here*.

We were exactly what he was seeking to star in his multi-million dollar campaign for the Los Angeles ready-made suit company; two chaps whose height – both above six feet – narrowness (ten inches at the widest point of the body, i.e., the feet) – arms dangling to just below the knee – were perfect to play the sort of misshapen customers whom only his client could fit off-the-peg. He made out draft contracts (noughts proliferated like frogspawn when money was mentioned) in the office of our BBC producer, Charles Maxwell. The American had to fly back to LA, by the afternoon Super-Constellation so Den and I had to be in Charles's office in BBC Light Entertainment's Aeolian Hall, Bond Street, the following day *not later than three pm*, to sign the contracts and become sincerely rich.

Denis lived then in a flat just north of Regents Park and I lived in a flat in Addison Road, West Kensington, near Olympia. We decided to take no chances at all. In the morning we would make our separate ways to the BBC canteen in Aeolian Hall, have a nervous lunch together in our best suits and – with plenty of time in hand – make our way up the staircase to Charles's office about half-past two, all ready to sign before three.

According to plan, Denis set off about half-past ten in the morning in his Morris, driving super-carefully round the north carriageway of Regents Park in an easterly direction. It was just as he was coming up to the Camden Town exit that he noticed, with a cold feeling in his tummy, that his right-hand trafficator was not working. When the lever was moved to the right to indicate that the driver was desirous of making a right turn, no illuminated arm sprang up – it had jammed. Denis did not panic – does he ever? He examined the problem and came to the correct conclusion. From then on he must turn only to the left.

His left trafficator up and throbbing, Den turned left and found himself proceeding north up the Holloway Road, a direction in which he had no wish to go. Bond Street was due South. It was alien territory to Den by then so he decided not to chance his arm on taking left turnings to God knows where but to proceed north towards Cambridge. His master-plan was then to *back* the car southwards from Cambridge. This would mean that a left-hand turn would, backwards, become a right-hand turn. He could then use a right-hand turn to back towards Ely, perhaps then working towards Bury St. Edmunds and down through Essex to London and Bond Street.

His scheme might well have worked but for the rain. Cars were then designed to go forward in all weathers but small provision was made by manufacturers for owners who had to drive a long way in reverse in inclement weather. There was no windscreen wiper on the rear window of Den's Morris and he could hardly see where he was going. In the small town of Ongar, in Essex, it all became too much. His rear window completely misted over and he inadvertantly, and at speed, backed up the ramp of a removals van, hit a three piece suite in uncut moquette and came to a halt. He raced to a telephone and explained the situation to Charles Maxwell at Aeolian Hall.

It was two minutes to three.

I, mid-morning, playing it safe, strolled up to the Kensington High Street end of Addison road to catch a bus to Bond Street.

The morning was sunny and as I waited I let my mind wallow in what it was going to be like to be extremely rich. Instead of three shirts I could have four; one on, one off, one in the wash and one to look at. The bus arrived and I climbed aboard. We could have grapes in the house even when nobody was ill. We could throw away the crust of bread which was beginning to go a bit hairy instead of, as usually happened, toasting it. Rather than rushing out and buying one little bottle of tonic water at a time I will be able to rush out and buy two. It was at about this stage that I realised that I was on the wrong bus.

Wrenched from my reverie, I focussed my eyes and saw through the window not the busy streets and shops of London's West End but cows. These flashed by and a sheepscape appeared, followed by quiet streets and a glimpse of a sign saying 'Woking Post Office'. Distraught, I leaped from the bus – before it had even come to a complete stop – and started running hard in what I believed to be the direction of Bond Street. A little way along I found a man on a tandem bicycle waiting at traffic lights for the lights to change. This was my chance – I would work my passage to Bond Street on the backseat of the tandem. The chap in front was all wrapped up in voluminous clothes, a flying helmet, goggles anda scarf round his face so in case the lights changed before I had a chance to explain myself I swung my leg over the back seat and climbed on. The lights changed. Away we pedalled.

We were speeding along merrily when I saw a sign saying 'Guildford – two miles' and realised that we were going the wrong way. I also realised that the chap in front had no idea at all that he had a stowaway behind him. I screamed in his ear but his silly helmet had flaps over his ears. I dug him in the back but his oilskins were too thick for the prod to register. So I just had to sit there. In revenge, I raised my feet and let him to all the pedalling.

As we arrived in Guildford we ran into a newly-tarred stretch of road and the tandem slowed almost to a halt. Seizing my chance, I slipped off the saddle and on to the tar – on terra firma at last. Very firma in fact. My shoes stuck to the tar and I had to dance lightly across to the pavement in my socks. It was then just a matter of finding an unvandalised phone-box, which only took an hour, and putting in an apologetic telephone call to Charles Maxwell in his office.

It was two minute to three.

In Charles Maxwell's office, Charles thoughtfully replaced the phone. The American producer looked at his watch and picked up the contracts he had laid on the desk.

'I have just two minutes before my car arrives to take me to the airport,' the producer said. 'Are those two guys going to get here in time?'

'I think not,' said Charles, sadly. 'They are both a long way away and not even together.'

'For Chrissake – where the hell *are* they?'

Charles sighed:

'Muir in Surrey, Den in Ongar.'

A little learning is a dangerous thing

Alexander Pope, An Essay On Criticism

Dear Mrs Henderson,

Let me first of all thank you for your very sympathetic letter. I shall deal with the problem you mention later, dear, but first – in reply to your kind enquiry – yes, I do still suffer from it.

In fact, only this week I was strolling through the Hosiery Department of Harrods when I saw a notice saying 'SUPPORT STOCKINGS'. Well, in the long-standing 'Stockings versus Tights' debate, it has never been a secret which side I favour, particularly as regards the black shiny ones. So, naturally, I hastened over to offer my support in whatever form it might be required. It was only when I reached the counter and noticed certain elasticised items of hosiery that I realised what had happened. I had once again fallen victim to that strange mental disorder about which you were good enough to enquire, Literalism.

What can I tell you about this distressing and time-wasting handicap? Psychiatrists describe it as 'A congenital inability to take words and phrases other than literally' – so that if, for example, a sufferer sees a cosmetic bottle with a label that says 'Lemon Rinse', the first thought that somes into his mind is 'Why on earth would anyone want to rinse a lemon?' Similarly, on first coming across 'Anchovy Paste', a Literalist will take it to be something used for mending broken anchovies. He will also spend a large part of his life wondering what 'Occasional Furniture' is the rest of the time.

What appears to happen, dear Mrs Henderson, is that the mental images conjured up by language, the interior pictures, are not the same for us as for other people. When I first saw the headline 'THREE ARMED MEN IN BANK RAID', for instance, my first reaction was 'Surely men with three arms would have more sense than to rob a bank? They must realise how *conspicuous* they'd be.'

But headlines are always a trial to those of us born with the unhappy habit of putting secondary meanings first. On being confronted with 'PUBLIC BORROWING DOWN', my instinctive response was 'What a strange thing for members of the public to be borrowing. Just shows how many people must be stuffing their own duvets.' And when I turned to the Arts Page and found a story headed 'HOCKNEY DRAWS LARGE CROWDS', the immediate thought was, 'Well, I suppose it must make a change from drawing swimming pools.'

'WOMAN HIT BY BUS CRITICAL' provoked the comment, 'Well, you could hardly expect her to be *approving*'; 'KILLER BELIEVED SPOTTED' merely summoned up a mental image of homicidal acne; and I would prefer not to elaborate on what went through my mind when I saw a Financial Page airline story with the heading 'VIRGIN EXPANDS'.

I wonder, though, if you can appreciate how irksome such misunderstandings can sometimes be. I need only quote a sign I saw in a shop window last January saying, 'SALE, LAST WEEK!' Mrs Henderson, I can't tell you how long I stood on that pavement in the pouring rain trying to puzzle out why they were bothering to advertise a Sale that had taken place seven days ago.

Sometimes it is the apparently self-evident nature of the announcement that arouses bewilderment, as happened with a kitchen supplier's advertisement I noticed not long ago in our local paper. 'STAINLESS STEEL SINKS' it said – and I can well recall how indignantly I greeted it. 'Was that statement really worth wasting good money on? I mean, not even a child would believe that it *floats*?'

But by far the greatest source of misinterpretation for those condemned to take words and phrases at their face value is the Public Notice. These can range from the increasingly common stickers saying 'NEIGHBOURHOOD WATCH' – for which the cinema inside my head never fails to screen a picture of local people popping round to see what time it is – to a little placard they used to have on certain Northern Line trains that read 'PASSENGERS ALIGHT BOTH ENDS'. As a boy, I can remember hanging about the platform for ages, without ever seeing one passenger's end as much as smouldering.

I hope this has helped satisfy some of your curiosity about Literalism, Mrs Henderson – a curiosity prompted, as you shyly mention on the very last page of your letter, by the fact that your husband recently, without any warning, and for no reason you can think of, walked out on you. Is there any possible way, you ask, that his unexpected defection could be attributed to a sudden attack of Literalism?

Mrs Henderson, as my psychiatrist so often says, one of the reasons why Literalism is such a little-known ailment is because so few people know about it. Therefore, my dear lady, I must answer your question by asking you to examine two things. First, your conscience; second, your washing machine.

I cannot presume to advise you about the former, but I do know something about the latter. If your machine is one of those that has a knob on it saying 'PULL ON, PUSH OFF', then you've got to be very brave, Mrs Henderson. As could so easily happen to someone suffering his first-ever attack of Literalism, your spouse gave the knob a sharp tug, then made his exit.

If that is the case, my dear, then we must face up to the fact that the hitherto unsuspected tendency towards Literalism lurking within him would have always put your marriage at risk. As an early Pope once nearly remarked –

'A literal leaning is a dangerous thing'